OPERATION ESPIONAGE:
THE SPY WITHIN

OPERATION ESPIONAGE:
THE SPY WITHIN

A Primer on Risk Mitigation

HARRIS SCHWARTZ

ISBN:	Hardcover	978-1-7960-7819-0
	Softcover	978-1-7960-7818-3
	eBook	978-1-7960-7817-6

Print information available on the last page.

Rev. date: 12/13/2019

To order additional copies of this book, contact:
Xlibris
1-888-795-4274
www.Xlibris.com
Orders@Xlibris.com
806168

CONTENTS

Preface

The purpose of this book is to provide the reader real-life examples of internal threats (spies in some cases) that could occur in most corporate enterprise environments. In some environments, these types of internal threats are prevalent over others just based on the type of business and certainly if your business handles, stores, uses, and develops/creates sensitive information, classified data, valuable intellectual property, trade secrets, etc. The book is also practical in that besides providing "short stories" of actual investigations conducted, I also provide a short analysis of the case (review) and suggestions on how to prevent, detect, report, investigate, and remediate these types of cases. This is a practical guide for all levels of risk, security and investigation management, and leadership. For confidentiality reasons, I have left out any identification of corporate entities described in each story.

Introduction

The news is blaring with cyber breach, cyber theft, and regulatory violations left and right. Many large well-known retailers have been the target of cyber attackers that exploited known vulnerabilities through a third-party supplier with the intent of compromising those systems and having access to a treasure trove of sensitive data that in the end game attackers will sell to the highest bidder and then they will move on to their next target or victim.

Insider threat can have multiple meanings. An insider (threat) could be a cyber attacker that has exploited some vulnerability and has been able to access your systems without authorization and now is inside your network (somewhere). Insider threat can also include an employee that has made the decision (willingly or not) to go rogue and cause some level of harm to your organization; the intent to steal information could be for financial gain. Insider threat can also culminate from well-organized campaigns by outside entities (sometimes referred to as a competitor), or it could be another government or agency of a government with an interest in your business, its executives, assets, etc.

Think of some of the well-known insider threat cases over the last ten years, with the onslaught of cyber breaches starting with retailers in 2013 due to third-party threat that allowed the attacker access into their network. In its simplest form, insider threat doesn't necessarily have to do anything with cybercrime—it's any type of insider that threatens an entity. There have been notable individuals working as a contractor with a third party doing business with governments. These examples of individuals had access to numerous files that they felt should be released to the public despite their data classification. There have been some insider threat cases that had nothing to do with theft and/or leakage of sensitive data; sometimes the intent was causing damage to a past client.

Chapter 1

State-Sponsored Insider

When I start the day, early morning on most days, I have a funny feeling that today is going to be an interesting day. My mind is always wandering and sometimes spiraling out of control, mainly because of the vastness of the corporate environment that is just under my fingertips, so to speak. As an experienced investigator, I work with many clients and is charged with a variety of tasks and responsibilities, including the not very familiar responsibility—counter-intelligence and domestic terrorism investigations, of which most of my peers could not say they were responsible for the same. The whole beginning of that topic will have to be told at another time.

I was hired by a company within the financial services field and had the opportunity to work with other teams at this particular client, some individuals who were charged with monitoring and auditing type of work. Many departments within this client were handling highly-sensitive work product and personal information, some of which were highly regulated, and other activities required close monitoring and tracking for a variety of purposes. In some cases, employees and their actions on a keyboard were tracked one at a time but included any button they hit on that keyboard. Keeping close details of worker activity was needed, especially in support of investigation.

Majority of my work at this client was actually dealing in large losses and what they dubbed as major crime, including organized crime, money laundering, and counterfeiting. My work took me all over the world as I was out chasing criminals wherever they led me to. On occasion, I had the request to put my solid skills and tradecraft to work on difficult-to-solve internal investigations. You will read about them later.

In this particular instance, I was working some external cases, and one of the interviews conducted with a suspect pointed to an insider that the subject was working with or, as he put it, information he was gathering from the internal employee as they were working together to mastermind some output that would garner them valuable commodity to the people they were actually working for—a *foreign* government. I began conducting background checks on our subject, including the "internal" employee that was finally identified by the subject. After a long interview turned interrogation, there was a joint investigation with the law enforcement.

Typically, when I start an investigation, I take the chance to run background and information check about the potential subjects/ suspects in the case. One of my glaring questions is, did they have a predisposition for a similar activity? The next part was inquiring around the company departments to understand if any of the subjects of the investigation (who may later turn to suspects) had accounts with funds and/or related activity, transactions, and personal/identifying information about themselves.

After a few interview questions with the external subject-which included visits made to his home, his workplace and his favorite bar that he frequented on a regular basis. I mean surveillance is one of my strong suits and an activity I greatly enjoy. Luckily, the external subject had a bunch of information that was found to be useful in the investigation and was still in his possession when last speaking to him at his home. On this particular event, I was alone (sans law enforcement). Working alone is usually helpful in many ways. In my position as a private investigator, I am able to do things that would normally require a search warrant or subpoena—protected by laws, which I always support and believe in. But I always cover my tracks and actions that if so required to turn over my notes or findings, all my actions are covered legally. As an example, in this case, the external subject consistently told me that he did nothing wrong and that I should be looking at the internal employee that was really responsible for the theft of information and other violations. So in appeasement with the subject, I asked him if he would consent to a search of his house. If he had nothing to hide, then why not consent, and doing so would go a long way in my report and discussions with the prosecuting agency. The subject agreed to my search of his home (as an individual but representing my client), and after his consent, I had him complete a handwritten note on a piece of paper (in his own writing) that he was consenting to the search by me, that he was not forced or coerced into the decision. I had him sign, date, and print his name on the document. Now I was covered should he try later (or his defense attorney) to rebut the home search, claiming violations of constitutional rights. Just so you know and realize, many of the tricks of the trade and "tradecraft" used in my investigations, especially those tied to criminal investigations, I had many a discussion with certain prosecutorial agencies to get by off on these tactics.

I conducted a search of the suspect's home in its entirety, and anything that I found of interest, I definitely put in an inventory with photo. This I did as part of an overall accounting of the items I was taking, in physical and virtual forms (e.g., photographs and videos), during the search. In the subject's office area, in plain view were documents that contained identifiable information of people other than the subject; some of which included Social Security numbers, account numbers, financial information, and other personal information, including driver's license information and, in some cases, passport documentation—clearly, not information that the subject should have access to, let alone be in his possession. After my search and inventory of items (photographs and any items I was removing physically), I showed them to the subject and again requested that he sign, print his name, and date a document acknowledging that he was aware of the items listed.

In some cases, I even ask the subject if he wishes to make a statement, and in this case, the subject wanted to make a formal statement. Of course, after I saw what I saw, why would he allow himself to be caught? For some, it's an innocent way to say they assisted in the investigation, and to others, it's just plain stupidity, but it happens. I informed the subject that since I was working on a joint investigation with law enforcement, the agents that I was working with were on their way over to his house for his formal statement.

We both waited indoors until law enforcement arrived. I wanted to make sure that the subject did not dispose of anything ("evidence") and that all was copesetic. They arrived shortly thereafter and entered the subject's home. We sat at the kitchen table, and as a formality, I informed the subject again that I was working on a joint investigation. Police started to advise the subject of his Miranda warning via a printed document of his rights and a place for his signature and printed name and date. The subject read the document, the agent read the subject his rights, and the subject signed the document. We then began the interview with the subject, sharing in on the questions and discussion to gather more information about his accomplice. All in all, the discussion lasted about ninety minutes. The subject was advised to get an attorney and was warned that he should turn himself in by nine o'clock in the morning. He was advised of the consequences if he would not turn himself in. He was also advised to not discuss the details of the day/ night with anyone else. This would also cause any deals to be made with the subject null and void. The subject agreed, and we departed the home.

The next morning, I met up with the law enforcement for coffee and to sync up on the investigation, review notes and other details, and the next steps to take. I turned over my notes and my subsequent details surrounding my home search conducted the night before. Our next step was to start looking into the employee (insider) that seemed to be the source of the information found in the possession of the subject. My next initiative was to reach out to my internal clients that could assist in gathering forensic data, keylogging activities, and other information on the employee—on confidential terms, of course. I also spoke with

HR to gather information about the employee, specifically documents related to his hiring and onboarding at the company. I wanted to review his identification documents as well as any additional information, like passport information.

Interesting enough and not surprising, the employee's passport at the time of hiring was of Asian origin. Apparently, the employee worked at a foreign office (same company) but was "on loan" in the United States for a specific period. I say "on loan" because that was the official request made by his superiors, not knowing or realizing the true reason the employee was able to pressure his superiors in Asia for the opportunity of "training" in the United States. Since the employee worked for the company, he was required to adhere to all internal policies, including the ethics policy, when it pertained to internal inquiries (and investigations). So I decided to schedule some time with the employee using a ruse of a meeting, asking for his help as we had an investigation into another employee that worked in his field and I needed information to help with my investigation. The employee agreed to meet and showed up for the interview.

The interview (ruse) was really meant as a way to perform a background on the employee, especially since we lacked info because he was a foreigner. I asked lots of personal questions about himself and his family and, of course, questions about his job and his duties (because his ruse subject worked in the same department) so that I could understand what systems and applications he used as part of his job or what activity he might be involved in on a regular/daily basis. These tidbits would certainly lend a hand in further investigating his activity internally and identifying areas of threat and/or areas where data loss might be occurring. The company subsequently had massive systems in place that allowed for monitoring and watching of any individual user on the network, at any time, no matter the location. The employee was overly helpful because as he stated he always likes to help superiors when asked, and so he was helpful in painting a better picture of himself and providing more avenues of discovery and approach for later use.

In the meantime, after parting ways with the employee and his apparent willingness to help out in the future if needed, it was important to perform some further research on the subject; myself, through other online resources and databases and through my law enforcement partners. First, wanted to get a better understanding of his travel, especially to the United State and from origin. The law enforcement was able to assist with information on the employee's origin (passport) and travel history (all travels were to/from the United States). Further information from other law enforcement agencies determined that the employee had ties to high-risk Asian countries and any activity may possibly be state-sponsored, that any schooling the employee was receiving in the United States was financially covered by a foreign government.

Bottom line, this employee was obviously circumventing hiring practices with the ability to be hired in a highly-regulated environment and further worked in a department that handled high-dollar transactions for a variety of customers; some with specific dealings between themselves and other entities, organizations, and governments—surely with some highly-valuable information. The employee was terminated from the company and sent back to their country.

Case in Review and Recommendations

While some of the aspects of the case and interaction between the employee and the identified external individual is not uncommon in this type of investigation (fraud/theft), it was determined (discovery) during the investigation that our primary subject (employee) did in fact have concrete ties to a foreign government. In retrospect, we had a foreign national that was not only employed originally at offices in Asia, but was also sent to the United States for training as a company employee. This is the point in time that the employee was involved in suspicious activity with the third party. It was severely alarming when I discovered the employee's allegiance with a foreign government, especially because of the highly-sensitive nature of the department that the employee worked in.

Recommendations:

1. Human Resources: I worked with a client's HR department to implement additional measures for any employees visiting/ interning/transferring from another country that was considered to be high risk. Although the individual was already an employee of the company (Asia office), HR modified their process to include information gathering and background checking (as applicable) for any individual originating from a high-risk country. This could clearly be designated by law enforcement. If the individual did originate from a high-risk country (higher risk in some designations), then corporate security would be notified for further review.

2. Travel Policy: The company had already implemented a travel security policy and process in conjunction with the Travel Services department, primarily for corporate security to be notified of any employee conducting business travel into a

high-risk country. The fact that subject employee worked in Asia, I was able to pull travel records overall for any business travel conducted by the employee, and in cases where travel was not booked through corporate travel (but personally booked), I was able to ascertain any travel to/from the United States.

3. HR and the Business Leader: The business leader in this case that accepted the short-term transfer of the employee did not make the "request" originally. Education and training was conducted with the business leader on steps he could take once knowledge of the transfer was occurring, in case there was any additional steps that should take place to further protect the company.

4. Vulnerability Management: Luckily, in this case, the subject employee did not bring his own laptop to the United States and thus plug into the network and install or introduce any malicious code. The client maintained a process and policy for any travelers originating from high-risk countries that once returning to the office, the help desk should be notified so that the computer could undergo a vulnerability scan before connecting to the corporate network.

5. Employee Interviews: The policy at this company was any investigations that included interviews of employees were conducted by corporate security/internal investigations without HR present. The investigations were governed by an extensive ethics policy that included employee requirements for participation in an investigation. The fact that the employee's origin was a foreign country, it is always recommended to check with your HR Business Partner to ensure you are adhering to any applicable employee laws for that country, whether the employee is in or outside the origin country at the time of investigational interview.

Chapter 2

From Russia . . . Not So Much Any Love

If someone were to tell me that there was a specialized group working at my client that was studying and defining new technology, services, and platforms for business customers and the fact that they were located in one of the most secure buildings under the most sensitive security systems and controls, I would have said no, not that I am aware. I always found out interesting things at my client from time to time, usually because others would bring them to my attention. My client would always tell me that employees would raise issues to him, and he always told them if they were bringing an issue to his attention, they should first present it as hypothetical because any issues brought to his attention by anyone would be required to be looked into immediately.

So my client called me on a Friday at 4:00 PM, and I was trying to decide whether I wanted to answer the phone or let it go to voice mail. Of course, I was kind of new working for this client and decided to answer it. My client's point of contact from their audit department was conducting a wireless audit of one of their facilities I mentioned above, and he stated that he was seeing things that he probably should not be privy to but were transmitted in the clear. I asked my client where in fact he was located, and he told me he was standing on the top floor of an adjacent parking garage with his equipment pointed at the building. I told my client I was on my way. I jumped into a taxi and told the driver to drive to the location as quickly as possible.

I arrived at the location, saw my client, and we walked into the secure building together. We met at the lobby, and he provided me with a location of where the data was leaking. I went and talked to the security manager at the check-in desk (as he had met me before), and I explained that I would be going up to third floor to check out the matter. I said, depending on what I find, there might be others arriving to address the matter and, in some cases, law enforcement. I also suggested that all individuals leaving the building should now be searched (bags and persons) until I provide an all-clear message. I went with my client up to the department and knocked on the door. I was let in by an unassuming smallish woman, and she said that her manager would be with me shortly. In the interim, my audit client was running some tests to see if he could identify the direct source of the leaks. I looked around the room, and there were probably about twelve people and workstations in the room, lots of electronic equipment and computer systems, two offices located toward the front of the room, and a large conference room toward the front door. The windows for the room appeared to be entirely blacked out with paper or other materials so that people outside would not be able to see in.

Shortly after, the manager approached and asked what my business in his room/area was. I asked if we could speak in an office, and he led the way. I identified myself with business card first and explained that my audit client identified suspicious activity originating from this area, which was contained within a secure facility, and the activity identified should not be happening. The manager asked how we were able to identify the activity, and my audit client provided context around his testing and audit and, essentially, that there were unauthorized wireless access points in this area that were not supposed to be in operation and, on top of it, not allowing anyone access to the sensitive data. The manager acted as if we were wrong and asked us to leave the area immediately or he was going to contact security. At this time, I identified myself with my credentials and instructed the manager that I would be conducting an investigation at this time and he and his team would not be able to leave the area until I was completed. I had a security guard from the lobby report to the area and to stand guard at the front door and to not allow any person to pass that did not have authority to do so. My client had to go to another meeting and asked that I would provide regular sitreps as much as possible. The client assigned a resource to assist me.

I had the audit resource walked around the room/area with his scanner to identify each of the wireless access points that were responsible for leaking the data. As he identified these workstations, which ended up being almost all of them, I contacted my point of contact (poc) within the cyber security group and requested they report immediately. Of immediate concern was the Internet connection in use by this group, and after digging into corporate records, it was found that the ISP connection was purchased by a team member using his own form of payment. Therefore, the ISP connection within the secure facility was never approved by the company (process) and not paid for using corporate funds.

I asked the manager to instruct all his employees to stop their work, to not turn off their computers, and to report to the conference room within the office area. Some of the employees were hesitant and remained working. I visited each of these individuals and instructed them to stop immediately and to go to the conference room. Several of the employees working in this area appeared to be of Eastern European descent. Majority of them were also speaking in a foreign language to one another in attempts to hide the context of their discussions. I reached out to a law enforcement partner that specialized in Eastern Bloc countries and asked if he could come over to the building in plain clothes to assist, which he gladly agreed. I asked my contact to sit in the conference room to listen to the conversations and to also be there for evidentiary purposes and eventually what would lead to criminal investigation at a later time.

While all the individuals were in the conference room, resources from Information Security were assessing the computer systems in the department, reviewing audit information gathered by the auditor scans and other forensic work. Next, I wanted to interview the manager alone, and so we used his office. The manager was not very accommodating, claiming he had deadlines to meet, and now with my "interference," he was going to miss the deadlines. In speaking with the manager, he informed me about the work that his department was responsible for. His group was only a small team of developers (of business-related applications), and as he told me and reminded me, he had this high-pressure project he was working on that he had hired additional people to augment his staff so he could hopefully complete the job faster. This was the first red flag as HR had no records of additional staff hired to work in this department. The manager was also fairly new to the company. The group of people that was hired by the manager were all of Eastern European descent. The manager was also of foreign descent and had "worked" with the Eastern European group in a past capacity.

All the temporary hires were interviewed to gather information about their understanding of the work required and the objectives of the project, and because none of them had undergone corporate process for hiring, they were unaware of the ethics policy and, therefore, could deny the request for an interview. Some of the individuals became hostile and wanted to leave the area. At this point, only having preliminary information about their work and suspicious nature of the work, I did not have enough evidence for law enforcement to administer an arrest. Those that wanted to leave the area were allowed, but their security access was terminated, and they were asked not to return to the office until notified. Physical security teams were also notified of these individuals and their current status for building access.

It was determined through further investigation and forensics that the manager and the hired individuals were tied to a foreign government and planted in the company for the purposes of exfiltrating data and theft of trade secrets, intellectual property, and customer data. The intent was building back doors into the business applications that would be utilized by business clients, and all their transactions and data would be copied and leaked through these backdoor locations. The Internet connection was, in fact, purchased by the manager (outside normal IT process and request) using his corporate purchasing card. Wireless Access Points (WAP) were set up in this office building with the purpose of development of the applications, connecting various equipment to the Internet connection, but also having the ability to connect from outside the facility, much like our audit team was able to do. The final case investigation report was referred to local prosecution officials for the district/region for prosecution.

Case in Review and Recommendations

The audit department the company had prior this instance just implemented additional auditing requirements for assessing wireless networks and access within the company buildings, especially within highly-sensitive and/or secure facilities. This instance of activity was an excellent finding by the audit department, and their quick action to contact corporate security was even a testament to our successful handling, response, and remediation of the issues. Many companies experience "shadow IT" operations and actions by non IT groups and/ or employees that think they have a faster way to accomplish a task that they require, but they do not want to follow procedures.

Recommendations:

1. Public and Private Partnerships - It is so vital to your work in security, risk, and/or investigations to have working relationships with law enforcement agencies. In some of my roles where investigations (external facing) were my primary responsibility, I found that certain law enforcement agencies would work jointly with you if you properly presented the case to them in a working partnership context. Some of my clients that merely "referred the case" to the law enforcement, let's say, didn't get any response.

2. Audit and Technology - Whether working in an IT role, information security, or corporate security/investigations, having a relationship with your internal audit group is key to success. There are various reasons for this way of thinking. For one, it's a great way to implement a new program or initiative that you can't proceed with simply because of lacking budgets or interest from your department. My clients have utilized their relationship with internal audit to influence the company to

move ahead with a particular project for the betterment of the company and all because internal audit usually gets their way. In other ways that are useful, similar to the situation in this story, their auditors know who to call if they spot policy violations, suspicious activity, and/or worse, criminal activity. Also, many companies have audit departments, but not all of them audit IT or technology programs. We all are aware of the risks of technology in the workplace, and having regular audits of this work is better for risk reduction overall.

3. Procurement - In this case, the manager was able to use their purchasing credit card for the purchase of Internet connection services for his area. It is important for risk management or corporate security leadership to implement education with procurement and purchasing groups on what I'd like to call "red flag purchases" so that if procurement or financial teams see purchases that meet the "red flag" list, then corporate security is contacted immediately. For one, this department should never have purchased Internet connections for their "office" without some sort of detection in place to identify this rogue connectivity.

4. Non-Employees - How did these hired individuals gain security access to this building in the first place? The company did maintain proper procedures that were tied specifically to HR systems that would supply the requisite request for employee access to systems as well as facilities. But I learned during this investigation that HR was not aware of the individuals nor where their names or information stored in HR systems, yet they all had access cards to grant physical access into a secure facility. Ensuring that all managers are aware and educated on company policy and procedures for new hires, temporary workers, and consultants is important. In this case, the manager was part of the fraud against the company, so even if he was fully aware of the company policy, he was not going to adhere to it. It was also determined that a security guard was "paid off" so that the workers could gain access to the facility.

5. Secure Development Life Cycle (SDLC) and Project Management Office (PMO) -Whether your company follows an agile, waterfall, or other development life cycle process, ensure that all business units in the company are aware and involved with following company process for the development of their applications and other projects. In this case, as previously demonstrated, the manager was circumventing process at every step, so there was no way that anyone was going to know about these applications or the developers or the back doors installed. The importance of ensuring that application code is scanned for vulnerabilities and includes developing concepts adhering to industry standards are important parts of any SDLC program. Information security or IT at the least should have programs in place that accomplish secure development of applications, constant testing and code scanning, and final reviews to ensure that privacy and security by design is implemented into the product or project.

Chapter 3

Corporate Espionage

In the scheme of things and based on all the movies you have ever watched over your lifetime, the simple definition of "espionage" as depicted in the best blockbusters is a government operative that infiltrates another government entity for the purposes of learning valuable state secrets. Yes, and this tradecraft is carried out by endless governments targeting other governments so they can learn their secrets. In the corporate sense of espionage, also referred to as industrial espionage, economic espionage, corporate spying, and just corporate espionage, similar to the latter, in that a person or group are spying for the purposes of gathering information (written, verbal, etc.) from another company, to better themselves competitively, financially or in some other way. In simple terms, corporate espionage refers to the taking of tangible property and/or intellectual property for the purpose of achieving competitive advantage in the marketplace.

According to federal law enforcement, the definition of economic espionage is foreign power-sponsored or coordinated intelligence activity directed at the U.S. government or U.S. corporations, establishments, or people designed to unlawfully or clandestinely influence sensitive economic policy decisions or to unlawfully obtain sensitive financial, trade, or economic information. There is a fine line between companies or entities gathering intelligence on their rivals; they all do, to some degree or another, but if activity goes too far, it could be defined as a criminal offense or two.

Many of the same actions taken by a computer hacker or attacker against a website would be defined as a criminal violation (US Title 18 Section 1029, 1030), and the same applies to corporate espionage. Here are some examples of actions that would be considered criminal:

- Trespass on private property
- Accessing competitor's files without permission
- Impersonating a competitor's employee (embedding individual as an employee, e.g., infiltrating an organization for the purposes of learning or accessing company trade secrets, sensitive information, protected information, etc.)
- Wiretapping or other recording device installation
- Hacking into competitor's computer systems, network, or infrastructure
- Installing malware on competitor's computer systems
- Implementing any type of cyberattack for the purposes of malicious activity (e.g., business e-mail compromise (BEC), phishing, spear-phishing, etc.)

As depicted in some of the previous chapters of the book and more to come, majority of everyday, run-of-the-mill corporate espionage occurs within the walls and confines of the corporation by employees, contractors, and other people that may have access to information that could be worth a lot of money to someone else. In some cases, those employees are disgruntled for one reason or another or even employees that are hired by a competitor to spy on your business. Many employees think they are welcome to customer lists and information because, after all, they worked hard to build these relationships, and why should they leave them behind?

As mentioned earlier in this chapter, sometimes foreign countries target U.S. corporations and undergo espionage activities of some level. It could be the foreign government is attracted to a company's new technology that is selling off the shelves of retailers around the world.

So that foreign government would like to copy that technology, reverse engineer and gain intelligence about the inner workings of the tech, so they can reintroduce a similar-looking and similar operating technology shortly after the company launched their product; now a company owned by a foreign government releases a new and emerging tech.

Chapter 4

To Live and Let Live in LA

I was often referred to as a competent investigator that could get the job done quickly and sometimes stealthy, dropping me into a location on short notice so that I could do what I do best, and that was to investigate and bring the investigation to a final conclusion within a very short period, typically within one week. The conclusion would either mean surrender of the subject, arrest of the subject, and/or identification of the subject responsible. Plusses for me and my work would be forfeitures of assets and/or recovery of stolen funds and/or assets that could be auctioned off to resolve some or part of the crime in the first place.

This issue dealt with internal employees at my client's company—about fourteen of them that were all working in a brick and mortar location. This was an interesting case in that the client's own in-house investigator had made an attempt to solve this case but went nowhere—no confessions, no arrests—but the visibility of this particular case rose to the top executive ranks in the region, and the bosses were not happy; hence, the introduction of another big case to work for this client that utilized me often.

I was always about collaboration and partnerships, especially in the whole context of public-private partnerships. In my line of work, it was so important to have these relationships. I always had my favorite law enforcement agencies that I preferred to work with. I agreed to take some of the "green" agents and perform some OJT at the same time.

This case was not like most because it involved (apparently) some internal bad apples that thought it would be easy to defraud the company as well as senior citizen customers. I often worked with the client's HR department, and in this case, HR gave me leeway and left the decision of maintaining/firing involved employees to me, based on the outcome of the investigation.

Upon landing at the airport, I reached out to my law enforcement contact, provided an overview of the case, allegations/criminal code violations, and key/primary subject. I coordinated a time and met up with the group at their office to plot out the next couple of days as the most important ones. HR had already placed the subject on administrative leave, which hurt our vantage point a little as we had to track him down. First stop was the office location to conduct interviews with the subject/associate employees that may have been involved. The company had a very strong ethics policy that included a "Miranda style" clause/notice to employees that were participating in an investigation, and with the requirement, their participation had to be honest and truthful as warranted. But as I chose to conduct a joint investigation, along with the law enforcement, on behalf of the client, this enabled the company's ethics clause to play a role with the associated employees while Miranda was also in play. It was like cutting out the middle noise and escalating to the most serious level so that the employees understood there were serious consequences if they were found to be part of the overall scheme.

We set up in a conference room at the brick and mortar location and called, one by one, each employee that was discovered to be part of the scheme in one way or the other. Between my top-notch interview/interrogation skills and law enforcement's, we were getting confession after confession as went down the line. This also enabled us to ensure each person kept the interview and details confidential, or else, additional charges could be added on to each. Once these were concluded, we decided it best to start working in the field to conduct the extensive investigation necessary, keeping in mind already-identified information, along with leads identified during the interviews.

Before I get into the field work, let me describe the overall case at hand. The company was receiving complaints from customers that money (in all sums and amounts) was missing from their accounts; sometimes a one-time loss and in some cases, over time. The average amount of each loss was about $15,000. It was determined that majority of the customers were senior citizens, at lease sixty years of age, and, in many cases, suffered from memory loss or other disease/defect that caused memory loss. The primary subject in the case was a senior employee, and he recruited two of his friends (non-employees) that would act as a customers that would eventually withdraw a large amount of money, in itself requiring additional steps and approvals for the money to be delivered from the central vault. The primary subject added his two friends as cosignatories onto two separate accounts and made requests for at least $100,000 each to be ordered for pickup by the "customer." The branch manager was the only person authorized to approve large dollar requests. The primary employee had sexual relations with the branch manager to win over her affection so he could obtain her credentials to approve the transactions. The other employees' involvement came similarly to the manager in that to make account withdrawal or bank transfers of $15,000, the primary employee also had personal relations with both men and women in the branch to obtain their credentials to process said account activity.

From the get-go, we had extensive information and leads about the case. Even prior to arriving at the airport, I requested the client's audit team to conduct transactional and keylogging reviews for this branch location (i.e., all employees) as well as any anomalies that may have been detected. We found that most customer transactions did not match or show the actual customer present at the teller counter and/or banker desk location.

The first piece of information we learned from one of the employees was that the primary subject had recently purchased a high-value vehicle for $85,000. We already knew the serial numbers for the cash that was ordered from the main vault, so if cash was used, we would be able to tie it to the subject. We located a small privately-owned dealer not far from where the target worked, where the subject purchased the vehicle for cash, paying it with crisp $100 notes, of which the sales manager thought was strange and so he kept a portion of the money just in case. Upon inspection of the cash left behind, we could determine that they matched serial numbers from the large cash batch delivered to the branch. Law enforcement seized the cash from the dealer. We could also ascertain further information, including license plate, VIN, and the fact that the vehicle was outfitted with on-demand services.

The next part of the investigation was taking into account some of the information we had gleaned from the interviews, along with additional leads of individuals that knew the subject employee. For example, we learned that the subject employee, although having sexual relations with most of his coworkers, was liking a particular coworker more than the others. In an interview of a coworker that was working at a different location, we learned that the subject employee had recently gotten into a fight with the husband of the female employee (lover); the employee was, in fact, married and having an affair with the subject employee. The coworker was aware that the husband of the lover came home early one night and found the two lovebirds in action in the bedroom. The husband chased the subject employee from the home with a crowbar. Once outside, the husband apparently struck the subject employee's new car with the crowbar, which apparently also caused extensive damage to the front and sides of the car, including the windshield. The subject employee was able to escape the enraged husband. The coworker told us that she was picked up by the subject employee, and they drove to a mall on the south side of town. While the coworker was doing some shopping, she mentioned the subject employee was going to drop his car off at an auto body business. The area around this specific mall was known for a number of auto body places within a one-mile radius of the mall. Even though the vehicle had OnStar device, we did not have a court order for OnStar to provide location, so we decided to do some old-fashioned detective work and visited auto body businesses looking for the subject's vehicle. After a few business locations, we came across a body shop and what appeared to be the subject's vehicle but covered with a tarp in an attempt to hide the identification of the vehicle. The body shop was closed by this point, so we took photographs of the alleged vehicle and its condition, and law enforcement reached out to the prosecutor for an emergency court order for OnStar to divulge the location of the vehicle. Within several hours, we received confirmation of the vehicle's location, both longitude and latitude, along with satellite imagery of the location. We returned to the body shop the next day to inquire with the owner on whether the vehicle was, in fact, on the property. The owner of the shop was not very friendly, and upon visiting the body shop, our strategy was to have me visit first to see if I could illicit the owner's involvement. The owner would not answer any questions and told me to get off the property or he was going to call 911. I told the owner that he was in luck, that law enforcement officers were here already; and that they would be happy to help. I requested law enforcement to come meet me and the owner. Right off the top, the owner asked if they had a warrant. Their reply was no, but they could get one, and it could become very ugly for his business, as they would need to shut down the business, police would be called to watch the owner and employees to ensure nothing was tampered with, and if it was found that he was working with criminals or involved in criminal activity, then other agencies would be brought in, etc. In the end, the owner said he would comply with our requests. We asked again whether the subject had dropped off his vehicle, and the owner did acknowledge this. Of course, we already knew based on OnStar information. The vehicle we had seen the night before covered in a tarp was, in fact, the vehicle. We asked to inspect the vehicle, and the owner did comply. At this point, law enforcement informed the shop owner that they were going to seize the vehicle and tow it to their facility. A warrant was issued for the asset forfeiture of the vehicle. The car was taken into custody. We asked the shop owner to contact his client and ask that he came down to the shop so he could review some repairs with him, but instead, we met with him to inform him that the vehicle was seized, and this was the first real opportunity for the subject to understand what he was up against. This was the first time he would be told (if he wasn't aware from some of his coworkers) that there was an investigation. The employee did show up, and we met with him briefly; at which time he said he had nothing to say and to leave him alone.

The next phase of the investigation was to identify his accomplices (non-employees) that were responsible for picking up the large amounts of cash, acting as customers, and helping the employee with his scheme. One of the previous employees that we interviewed mentioned the subject employee having a close friend that worked at a local coffee shop. We knew what the friend looked like since we were able to review past CCTV of the money pick-up. We went to the local coffee shop but found that the individual was off for the day, but the manager gladly provided law enforcement with his home address. We visited the individual's home with the intent of interviewing him to gather information about the investigation and subject with the hopes of a confession from the individual. The individual did allow us to enter his home. We were at the home for about four hours, mostly talking and trying to get the individual to admit to his part in the investigation, and there was a promise of immunity for his cooperation. By the end of the third hour, the subject employee showed up at his door. The employee was not surprised to see us there and asked us to leave his friend alone. As part of the investigation, we had previously showed up at the subject's home with a voluntary request that he allow us to search his home, but he declined. Now at his friend's house, he was driving his personal car. We asked whether he would allow us to search his car in his presence. The subject allowed us to search his car. We wrote out a statement for the employee granting us the right to search the car; at which time the employee signed the paper. Myself and one of the law enforcement officers entered the vehicle to search the center console and glove box for any evidence of criminal activity. The glove box had no documents or information, but the center console contained an excel spreadsheet copy that was folded up into a tiny square that when unfolded, revealed names, personally identifiable information like Social Security numbers, driver's license numbers, bank account numbers, etc., which were all customers of the company. Having this information in his possession was a felony in itself. We had to detail and catalog any evidence or material we were seizing from the car and show that to the employee so he understood what we were taking. At this point, the employee realized he was in a bad situation. We informed the employee that it was in his best interest to surrender and he had until 9:00 AM the next day to do so. He agreed, and we left.

Knowing some information about the subject employee and his tendency to try and hide and evade police capture (based on other information during interviews), it was decided that a BOLO—be on the lookout—would be released to regional law enforcement officials in the surrounding counties in case the employee had decided to evade rather than surrender, just thinking ahead of the employee and any actions he may take to evade. The next morning came, 9:00 AM went, and no employee. At about 9:30 AM (at the same time police were obtaining arrest and search warrants for the employee), I received a call from an attorney representing the employee, and she asked if we could meet her and the employee at her office, where the employee wished to surrender and provide a full written statement of his actions. It turned out that the employee was going to run but went to his attorney's office instead. We drove and met with the attorney and employee. He did surrender, and he did confess to his actions.

CHAPTER 4

Case In Review and Recommendations

This case was an interesting one. As an investigator working with my client, my primary responsibility was typically assisting the client with all types of investigations, both involving internal employees and third parties. Initially, this investigation was handled (improperly) by another investigator that, in my opinion, didn't do their job as best they could with the information at hand. The goal in security or investigations is to mitigate the risk before it turns into a major issue for any company. Once the awareness and visibility of an issue makes its way to center stage and executives are now aware, it becomes so important to nip it in the bud as soon as possible. Of course, at that point, the higher-ups are not only looking for a favorable ending that benefits the company but one that also reduces their risk exposure.

There were so many things that went wrong at an employee-to-employee relationship level and certainly much to do with a breach in ethics everywhere you look. The manager should have known better to not involve herself in a personal romantic relationship with her subordinate. The manager also lacked skills in knowing what her employees were doing on a daily basis and just overall operations of her business. These issues were not necessarily the responsibility of the investigator to determine, but many of these vulnerabilities were identified during the early stage of the investigation. In the end, majority of employees, including the manager, were not processed criminally but were, in fact, terminated from the company.

As I and many of my clients in their environments have learned, there are always employees that find the need to try and circumvent the process, "game" systems with an attempt to benefit them personally and actions that rise to the level of mistrust, theft, fraud, and other criminal behavior.

Recommendations:

1. New Hire Orientation - It is important to ensure that new hire orientation includes areas of theft prevention, specifically informing employees of the result if they try to defraud the company.

2. Manager's Responsibility - Security and/or other groups should ensure timely awareness activity with managers so they are aware of their responsibilities when it relates to their employees, especially with the use of company systems and in cases where customer data is in use.

3. Proper Procedures - The company, in fact, had proper procedures for most actions requiring approvals; in this case, the ordering of a large sum of cash. Having proper process, standards, policy, procedures, and guidelines will help ensure all employees are carrying out their business activities as approved by the company. There could be additional measures put in place in this instance, i.e., authentication measure involving the primary account holder to ensure their request is legitimate.

4. Ethics Policy - Many larger corporations maintain a detailed ethics policy that includes concepts surrounding company investigations and the involvement by employees and their requirements for involvement. This is just another step for employee compliance within the company.

5. System Auditing - If your business is highly regulated and/or the data that you work with is highly sensitive, then it is a good idea to deploy and implement internal auditing systems and tools to ensure all employee activity is logged and captured. Having the ability to review logs and data related to activity in the past is important as well. Logging of data and activity can be a compliance and/or contractual requirement, so always confirm with your risk, compliance, and/or legal department.

Chapter 5

How Not to Spend Corporate Money

Excessive spending gone awry—takes me to another client, and boy did they seem to have lots of internal fraud, especially by employees and some that were very creative in the way they managed company money. It does not surprise me one bit as I look back on my career to be bothered by the amount of internal dishonesty, fraud, and manipulation that carries on at most companies. In this particular case, one of my clients from accounting contacted me because she received a suspicious phone call from their corporate credit card company outlining that a certain employee had recently made a high-dollar purchase using his corporate credit card while visiting Germany. I gathered the initial information and then began my investigation.

In contacting an investigator contact at the credit card company, she proceeded to inform me that the employee was on a business trip in Germany and had visited the local high-end luxury car manufacturer factory to purchase a $100,000 vehicle. At first, I was thinking about the client's executive protection crew, and I knew they had not decided to make any further purchases, as the fleet was well positioned with what they had. Plus, this employee would have nothing to do with purchasing a vehicle, based solely on his position of working in IT. So I was able to gather information about the purchase, the vehicle and the delivery date for the vehicle, which was to happen in the United States at a designated dealer close by the corporate HQ. We wanted the delivery to occur, so I informed the investigator at the credit card company to ensure that the delivery happens and to make sure a representative reaches out to their client to schedule a delivery time.

I went and discussed this issue with my client to advise him of the investigation and that I was going to initiate a formal investigation into the employee. I was granted approval, so I went off on my escapade. I usually run a background check using one of the many public database providers. They were all pretty much the same. I did this so I could determine if the subject (employee) had any prior disposition for criminal/civil activity. I usually did not limit it solely to the state where the HQ was located but ran a national criminal check. I also contacted my POC in HR to see if they had a recent credit report pulled on the employee, as it was customary to run this report annually, especially for certain positions at the company. This employee was of senior leadership, so a credit report would be ran. In fact, HR had a recent copy, and upon review and analysis, it appeared as if the employee was spending a lot of money, even past the point of what the employee should have been able to spend at his salary. This was a good mental note.

Next, I would typically pull security monitoring logs for the employee in question to get an idea of their Internet habits at least, any suspicious websites that they may have been visiting while at work using corporate resources. This activity seemed pretty normal, except for a few unsavory websites that appeared to be pornography sites. I jotted down the website names for further analysis and review later. Being that this investigation involved misappropriation of corporate money and because this employee managed a budget, I reached out in confidence to our controller and requested a copy of all department budget items for this employee's department. I reviewed the budget, and I say it's pretty organized, not too bad, as I have seen much worse in the past. Maybe at a different juncture in this book, we'll see. Upon review of the budget under telecommunication line items, I noticed the employee had line items for numerous T1 lines, which seemed strange only because our networking group bought, installed, and budgeted for any communication lines for the company. So I needed to look further into these three T1 lines. In contacting the networking department, I was made aware that the employee purchased the lines using his budget money and using these T1 lines for his home residence. Networking simply stated that the employee told them that because of his position with the company, he required the extra bandwidth at home for after-work hours, emergencies, and such. Of course, one T1 line would be plenty for any amount of after-work hours. This guy had three of them—definitely strange and suspicious. I was merely trying to collect as much information as possible so I could conduct the employee interview successfully.

I decided to go back and look into the porn sites that I had noted the day earlier. In analysis and review of WHOIS and other data, I was able to determine that the three porn sites all were owned by an LLC group in the same city as the HQ. I had to do some further digging with public records to try and identify people related to the LLC and ended up driving down to the courthouse and county records building to perform some searching. I was usually pretty good at tracking entities, money, and people down. Anyway, I was able to finally tie the LLC to our subject (employee) in this investigation. It made sense as to why he needed three T1 lines in his home, got me thinking even more.

I ended up reaching out to the client's audit department to ascertain whether or not the employee's expense records had been audited recently. They had not, so I requested the last few months so I could include them in my review/investigation. I had wanted to see if he was using his corporate credit card for other purchases that would be deemed non-business-related and/or violating company policy. Sure enough, his expense reports read as if he was a sales guy in the organization. I know salespeople tend to get a bad name because they try to stretch applicable spending and entertainment expenses when entertaining a client or not with a client. I have seen some great attempts—escorts, gentleman's clubs, motel rooms, etc., kind of topic for this investigation. His expense reports looked as if he were buying gifts, expensive ones, for someone, e.g., ten high-end crystal vases. I mean, how many vases does one person need? So I took some notes and made some copies, handed the reports back to audit, and informed them they should begin audit procedures at some point for this employee. Audit agreed.

In the end of this investigation, it was time to interview the employee. He did confess to the entire charade identified. This was an employee in a powerful management position in a company that did not pay close attention to the activities of their employees. We did solicit law enforcement interest in this case, and they did end up arresting the employee.

CHAPTER 5

Case in Review and Recommendations

This particular case was consistent in parts with many companies in the 1990s to early 2000s that lack foresight, audit, process, and procedures and overspent to the detriment of the company. The subject of this case was a mid-level executive running a department within an IT organization and had a lot of influence with C-suite executives and other management throughout the company. The mantra at this company was to allow managers and even employees to "go and do their job" with less management babysitting. Because the subject worked in IT, he had greater control and access to telecommunications products and services and was easily able to obtain products for his own use without anyone knowing. Sometimes it's being in right place and at the right time because in this scenario, a third party was concerned at the magnitude of the business purchase and wanted to confirm the activity with the company to ensure it was a legitimate purchase in the first place. Great on the credit card company for being proactive to reduce risk if, in fact, the purchase had turned out to be unauthorized.

Recommendations:

1. At the start of this investigation, there was no formal audit program in place. Most companies today will have some level of risk management or audit department for compliance reporting and auditing. It was certainly helpful to have another third party to provide advisory to this situation, which was a direct result of the investigation in general. In this case, the auditing of expense reports was necessary as there was extensive violations of company policy, even though department managers were signed off on employee expenses, no matter the type of expense.

2. In the case of ordering telecommunications equipment for the employee, this investigation found that improved processes and

approvals were necessary to prevent the sort of abuse that was identified with this employee. There is a need for checks and balances at all times.

3. Charging Limits on Corporate Credit Cards - Although the credit card company did proactively reach out about the business charge, the company should implement charging limits for all employees and managers, depending on their level within the company. This aspect was missing from the process of opening a business credit account for employees.

4. Better Control over Spending - Unfortunately, not too many managers or leaders in the company were concerned about the expenses reported by their employees, even though proper policy was in place at the time.

5. Acceptable Use Policy for Employees - A limited policy was in use, but it did not extend out to "consumer or business" products that were appropriated to employees as a benefit. It is necessary to hold employees to the same, if not more policies, around acceptable use of networks, computers, and other peripherals at all times, to limit risk and liability to the company as a whole.

Chapter 6

Cyber Espionage

In an earlier chapter about corporate espionage, I provided some examples of espionage activity. Cyber espionage is similar in that the spies are attackers, hackers, and other malicious bad actors representing themselves, foreign governments, and other entities that deploy and employ the use of advanced threats, cyber warfare, and technical tradecraft through deliberate and sometimes elaborate cyberattacks for the purposes of stealing protected, sensitive, classified, or intellectual property from corporations, governments, military, and other entities.

As citizens of the United States, we have seen and/or heard of many examples of cyber espionage, specifically in the 2016 U.S. presidential elections, interference by entities allegedly tied to foreign governments. Part of this interference was the manipulation and exploitation of known vulnerabilities in connection with voting software and hardware in various states. Some of these states were utilizing outdated programs and software, and in other cases, these same systems were years overdue for vulnerability updates and other countermeasures to protect "democracy" in the United States. Since I am on this subject of vulnerabilities, common-day hackers and attackers are constantly "knocking" on the doors of corporate websites and applications looking for known vulnerabilities that have not been patched or upgraded and would now be susceptible to an attack or exploitation. In some cases, cyberattacks target new technology and/or areas within society that are known to have some flaws. In this sense, Internet of Things (IOT) has busted the seams of corporate entities globally and, in many cases, confronts the real-world issue of attackers and malicious actors simply because the entity with IOT hasn't been able to address this issue. IOT has become a rampant risk in several notable cases, especially with smart devices. These devices usually have default passwords from the manufacturer that cannot be changed by the consumer, as well run certain exploitable protocols (e.g., plug and play) which then has enabled groups of attackers (hackers) the ability to takeover devices (zombie) and form botnets out of these smart devices for the purposes of launching distributed denial of service (DDOS) attacks that have shut down some of the largest web addresses in the corporate world.

Five to ten years ago, there was a handful of foreign countries tied to cyber espionage activities: USA, China, Korea, and Syria. According to UK's GCHQ, they recently estimated that there are thirty-four nations that now have serious and well-funded cyber-espionage teams targeting nations and other entities on a regular basis. Since there are so many nation states with well-proportioned and active cyber teams, this means that corporations and other entities will need to have a fully-functioning incident response team, along with an incident response plan, as well as ongoing testing of the plan and scenarios. Working together with your stakeholders in a crisis is similar to incident response—it's having an exact plan of who to call, what are the steps necessary to triage and investigate the incident quickly, and then how to remediate and further mitigate the issue from recurrence.

All entities with computer systems that connect to the Internet should already be in the mind-set of already "being under attack or compromised." It would be negligent for any entity to think that because nothing has happened to them now, why spend money and resources on cyber security? If nothing is happening against your Internet-connected computers, then it's likely your entity isn't doing enough to know (visibility) what is happening inside your networks and computer systems. At a minimum, monitoring of key systems and critical assets are important to healthy cyber security posture for your organization.

There is a host of tools, technologies, security applications, and the like that go into securing your networks and computers and protecting your assets from unauthorized access, disclosure, and theft.

Over the last couple of years, news have highlighted a specific tactic of attackers and hackers hired by mostly foreign governments and nation states to target MSPs (managed security providers) for very specific reasons. But I am not talking about the larger MSP companies; these nefarious bad actors are targeting small to medium businesses (SMB) and mom-and-pop-style shops for the following reasons:

1. Small- to medium-sized businesses typically do not employ the same numbers of cyber security staff and, in many cases, utilize IT personnel to perform security tasks.
2. Just like in most application style attacks, where attackers are looking to exploit known vulnerabilities, evidence has found that many of these no-name, unknown MSPs have unpatched networks and out-of-date programs and non-updated systems where vulnerabilities are found.
3. Most of these MSPs provide managed security services for a variety of companies of all sizes and typically maintain ongoing privileged access (mismanaged) into their client's systems. All it takes is an attacker breaching security at an MSP, and now they have full access to their client's sites where there could very well be sensitive information that could be detrimental to their clients if it has gotten into the wrong hands.

With the continued growth of the cyber security industry, there is a proliferation of numerous MSPs that are coming out of the woodwork, many providing "specialized" services for a specific issue, e.g., PCI-DSS requires a specific list of compliance requirements, so a good number of these MSPs will outbid the larger players, but in the end, they will fail to have the ability to scale upward to meet client demands and requirements. Companies on budget, looking to save, should include assessment processes and protocols to ensure the MSP is up to snuff and up to task to support all your long-term needs.

Chapter 7

Why Security by Design Is Best for Applications

I am sure that most IS professionals are tired of hearing about concepts like "privacy by design" or "security by design," but in reality, many companies and organizations fail to ensure that applications (e.g., web, mobile, etc.) are properly and securely written (coded) and checked/verified that the code is free from errors and security issues like vulnerabilities. After all, most types of attackers with any ounce of experience are always looking for the easiest way into an organization, e.g., exploit a vulnerability in an application or system, among other ways, of course.

You are probably wondering how this applies to a spy or internal threat situation. Well, as corporate security professionals, we always seem to get involved in some crazy at times issues, and this was clearly one of them. I had a client in the pharmaceutical space that I worked with a long time ago for a variety of issues/reasons. In this particular case, the client was upset and baffled that a competitor always seemed to know firsthand and oftentimes confidential information about business operations that, in the wrong hands, could be detrimental to the business.

I brought in other partners to this case, including forensics specialists and other network SMEs, to fully understand the dynamics of the client's network and infrastructure and then had the long task of tracking and tracing suspicious traffic, anomalies (network-related), net flow data, packet capture logs (PCAP), and other user behavior activity. We had to install special tools that the client was not utilizing at the time. Of course, hindsight 20/20, if the client had implemented some of these tools, then it would have been easier for us and them to become wise of the activity in the first place.

First, we started to look at network traffic and identified patterns and what we thought were suspicious activity outside of what we identified as normal daily or nightly traffic. Since the client had many processes and tasks that would run automatically through the day and often at night, we needed to determine what traffic was approved and what traffic fell in the realm of suspicious, requiring further investigation. This was a daunting task as the client had little to no information about their network, applications in use, daily and nightly processes, etc. We had to take a whole new stance and direction with interviewing all their business stakeholders so we could understand what activity related to them via the network. We reviewed outbound firewall traffic as well to determine (or had to) where traffic was headed and whether it was authorized or not.

What we ended up finding out was interesting in itself. A certain business unit had hired (recently to this case) a new application developer for a high-profile business application that was apparently tied to statistics and performance. This group was given carte blanche most times when it came to anything—requests, changes outside of a change window, no CAB, no SDLC, etc. In speaking to the hiring manager/business stakeholder, we asked some initial questions regarding this new developer, things like where did he come from, was he referred to you, referred by someone else, etc. That initial inkling of the origin of this employee was on our minds. We kept this initial discussion very short, but we needed some important basic background information. I contacted the HRBP for the business unit and requested new hire paperwork for the employee for further review. Nothing really stood out, at least not what I was expecting or surmising I might see, something in the lines state-sponsored activity, etc., but what I did see after further review was a consistent background of employment with other companies in the same industry as the client. Now what would be so interesting with that, right? Most people with industry experience end up working for similar companies in their work lifetime. Something didn't look right, so a deeper dive into social media, I went looking for more information. A few days later, bingo! This employee had developed a similar application at another client. Hmmm. So I reached out to my contact at that company to inquire about the employee and what they knew about him and his circumstances of not being employed any longer. It took a bit of time as my contact was traveling and such, but we finally caught up. The employee was terminated because of intellectual property theft. The company never proved how the employee stole the information, except for some preliminary computer forensics evidence showing some suspicious activity and the knowledge that data did go missing.

We continued on with our investigation, forensics, network traffic review, and such to gather more information and leads we hoped. Now we started to define suspicious traffic patterns that were occurring during an interesting time frame in the middle of the night, between 2:00 AM and 3:00 AM. Now, at first, we thought it could be legitimate traffic because often business units will run processes and tasks during off hours so that most importantly they are not hogging the bandwidth. Now that we had this pattern night after night after night, we could then start drilling down and tracing the traffic through the network and outbound through the firewall to its final resting place. We also performed some research on any changes or requests to the firewall configuration to allow this traffic (a.k.a. whitelist), and we did find that about four months prior and close to when the employee began employment with the client did they make a formal request (through the ticketing system) to whitelist their application traffic to a third-party website. The request was never really reviewed or investigated by anyone but simply approved by an engineer.

All in all, the investigation determined that the code developer responsible for this application was not what it was intended for but instead developed to act as a trap-and-trace device deployed on the network to gather legitimate business information and then exfiltrate the data to their third-party repository, where the information was downloaded and taken. This was running for months, and it had gathered information that was being leaked to a competitor that was ultimately helping that competitor engage in business decisions that undermined the client for the competitor's benefit. We have all seen steps people will take for competitive advantage and information gathering, but this activity sunk to a criminal activity that was both intentional and malicious to the client. We had to ensure a couple of things before we took down the application, stopped the traffic flow, and put an end to this malicious insider. We were able to feed it false information for a couple of days, so that legitimate information was no longer leaving the client's network. I was able to obtain interest from the local prosecutor for the region to prosecute the malicious insider along with the "company" that hired him to perform his work. Arrest and search warrants were signed by a judge, and the CEO of the company in question along with the malicious insider were met with a 6:00 AM wake-up call at their respective residences.

Case in Review and Recommendations

This was the type of case that haunts companies that work with or create/develop highly-unique intellectual property. If things get in the wrong hands, it could seriously affect their business. As security professionals, you sometimes hear about the competition of your company and the lengths they will go just to be ahead of the competition. In this case, the industry was biotech. The way the client company found out about the situation was through an ex-employee that had gone to work for a direct competitor to a product the client was developing for specific medical issue. The ex-employee had worked specifically on the project in question and being at the competitor, started to come across data and materials that looked familiar. This was a complete coincidence for this client and the fact their ex-employee with knowledge came across what she knew as specific data that was written by people she knew at the client company. Then the question was, how was the client data making its way to the competitor's hands? If it wasn't for this ex-employee, the client company would have never known that their competitor had their information.

Recommendations:

1. Data Protection Strategy - In businesses that rely on their intellectual property to do business or work with sensitive data that should be protected at all times, it is important to develop a comprehensive data protection policy and standard for the company. This standard can be a framework in which the organization works from that describes the details of how data should be protected to prevent unauthorized access and/ or disclosure of protected data and policy in which employees need to remember when working with new products or services that might touch this sensitive data or intellectual property.

One great way to do this is through a technology called data loss prevention (DLP), which can be utilized for e-mail communications and network traffic.

2. Security Monitoring - Either deploy your own SIEM (security incident and event manager) to log various devices and appliances in your environment so that there are "eyes on glass" with regard to continuous monitoring for security events and incidents or hire a third-party MSS (managed security services) provider to do it for you. Having proper levels of visibility into security activity within your organization is highly important. Plus, it meets many compliance and/or regulatory requirements.

3. Secure Development Life Cycle - Similar to other situations previously discussed, have proper process in place to ensure applications are developed with security and privacy in mind. It is also important to have relationships with your business unit stakeholders to ensure you understand everything there is to know about their business and projects to ensure security is addressed every step of the way.

Chapter 8

Corporate Assets for a Reason

Most organizations, companies, and government entities have and provide some level of computer assets that are deemed for business purposes only. These assets come in all forms: phones, tablets, laptops, desktops; you get the picture. Usually, employees are required to sign some form of policy statement regarding their assets and use restricted to business only, including the fact that one should never share their credentials, especially their password, etc. But, as risk managers or IS professionals, we all know this (sharing) happens all the time, or employees use their work assets for personal business, e.g., online web surfing.

As a long-standing professional working in the security field (and that is wide and vast in itself), I have certainly come across my fair share of incidents, security events and issues that sometimes found me holding my head and shaking it abruptly. No hair to really pull out. In this particular case, while working for a consumer-products client, I found myself alerted to suspicious traffic and activity (namely failed logins) related to a large number of highly-confidential servers that were utilized for payments and PCI-DSS activities. Only certain few with business need had access to these servers, and on top of it, the servers were hidden away (somewhat) on a separate V-LAN infrastructure. But in this case, a certain computer was originating large amounts of traffic to these servers, for thousands of attempts over a ten-minute burst every hour for eight hours in the wee hours of the night.

The client's network engineering team was the first to identify this activity through ongoing NOC operations. One of the struggles we face in this industry is the numerous amounts of traffic that traverse networks and infrastructures at all times of the day and night, by the sheer number of business groups and technology in play, so the arduous task of identification of traffic that is normal and authorized versus unauthorized and suspicious is an ongoing task for IT, network admins, and most times security as well. The network team had deployed variety of technology throughout the network to best watch areas of the network that could be prone to insider and/or malicious traffic, e.g., east-west traffic as many like to call it. After all, if you have an attacker that has been in your network, sitting idle and waiting for the opportune time to strike, east-west traffic is usually where you will find them and their tracks. Sometimes attackers can be in your network for months at a time, and if you don't deploy proper tools, then you'll never know they are there.

We started to examine the net flow traffic to determine what we were looking at. Yes, we did confirm a constant barrage of login attempts to the protected PCI servers, and we were able to identify the username that was responsible for the traffic. It was a surprise that the username belonged to an HRBP assigned to retail employees, so we thought it could be the user did, in fact, have access as some of the servers were utilized for statistics and such, and possibly, the HRBP needed access or had access, but maybe they were fat-thumbing the login. Anything is possible these days. So I was on a mission to speak to the HRBP to understand their role a little more and what servers they might have access to, like these PCI servers, for special reasons. I met with the HRBP to conduct an information-gathering session and, through the interview, learned that the HRBP has "never" had access to these servers, and she didn't know why her computer was trying to access them. I also asked if she had ever let anyone else use her computer at any time, and her response was very defensive (since she was HR) that I would think that she was violating policy and attempting to access servers that she was not authorized to access. I thanked her and went on about the investigation.

Given the answers and responses I received from the employee (HR), It was now time to understand better or more effectively why her computer was acting this way. I requested that IT contact the user and swap it out for a loaner as some testing was necessary on her computer. The computer was picked up by IT, and still not knowing what we were facing, I tended to use investigative process at all times. Chain of custody and evidence seizure was underway and well documented. Next, it was decided that forensics was necessary on her computer and, simultaneously, also started reviewing proxy log and firewall traffic to understand and identify any patterns of use by the user.

Prior to making a forensically sound copy of the hard drive, I requested IT to run a scan of the machine to ascertain if there was any malware or other bugs on the computer. The scan showed no such buggy activity, so that was ruled out as a possibility. Forensics was conducted and completed, and there were some interesting signs of misuse and some applications that were not approved to be used on the work asset. But it was a bit strange because this HR employee was not very technical, but the applications found would indicate the user would require top-level technical abilities. This fact started to sway my thoughts that there was another person using the computer.

Through good old-fashioned log, PCAP, and proxy review, we were able to identify the username and some of the characteristics of the additional person that was utilizing the computer. It was not, in fact, the HR employee, but it turned out to be her cousin that she allowed to use it. There was extensive web usage that indicated the cousin was tied to organized hacking groups that did not like this company, and the cousin of the HR employee utilized the computer on numerous occasions at the employee's home and at various cafes. The user was deploying various hack-as-a-crime tools to target the PCI servers and attempting brute force access by having access to employee records, figuring someone would have access to these servers, and the cousin could continue his malicious activity. But the users with access to these sensitive servers were required to utilize a variety of access control standards, and just a username and password was not enough; hence, the nontechnical understanding of the HR employee. The cousin had to have knowledge and information that only the HR employee had access to, and through traffic analysis and forensic investigation, it was learned that the employee was complicit in the activity, including the preparation and planning of the "attack."

In the end, the attack traffic was unsuccessful to this malicious activity. The employee was interviewed and terminated immediately. The case was referred to local law enforcement for advisement about the cousin, in case there was subsequent cases regarding the individual.

Case in Review and Recommendations

This was a case that involved malicious activity by both an employee (in a respected position) and an associate with a primary intent of causing financial loss to the company (economic damage). It was unfortunate to find that the employee's associate was really the person with malicious intent, and they were able to influence the employee to assist them in their campaign against the company.

Recommendations:

1. Acceptable Use Policy - This company did have and enforced an acceptable use policy among other policies that governed the use of employee credentials, Internet usage, and what activity was acceptable and not. This employee, being an HR professional, thought she was above the "corporate policy" and, as we saw, violated the policy time and time again. HR employees should know better, and this one did not. AUP or acceptable use policy started back in the early 90s with the widespread acceptance of the World Wide Web and the Internet (what we think of it today). The AUP was a way for Internet service providers (ISPs) to provide requirements of its users (while using the ISP) and essentially policy with oversight. The ISP typically had a terms of service (TOS) as well to govern the same about users. Companies took interest in ensuring that while employees utilize corporate assets, Internet and other tangible interests, that the company now had a way to also govern and enforce a policy that was specifically tied to employee activity. Nowadays, with the combination of an AUP, ethics policy, and information security policy, companies are well protected and have provided much notice to their end users.

2. User Behavior Analytics (UBA, UEBA) - In the last several years, there have been numerous security vendors that have provided/offered user behavior analytics type tools to be used on a network (infrastructure, usually corporate) to measure normal user risk versus elevated (out of the norm) risk and then provide tools, alerting and metrics for incident responders, threat hunters, SOC analysts, etc.to determine whether the alerted activity was normal or not. This is definitely a must-have tool in the toolbox, especially for any enterprise that deals in sensitive/protected/regulatory data. You can feed data from your UBA tool into a larger SIEM or not and have threat hunters specifically use UBA as stand-alone.

3. SIEM Logging and Alerting - Monitoring various applications, systems, servers, and devices on your network is vital so that you have the full picture of your enterprise. Failed logins is something that happens *all the time*, and many that do monitor security events on their network decide to skip events that create too much noise. Failed logins is not one of those noisy alerts that you simply want to skip or forget.

Chapter 9

Risk Assessments

As you have read, there are a whole host of scenarios that can plague any entity, whether private/public corporation, military, and government entities. The one aspect that is consistent across all industries is the term risk assessment. First off, any new "chief" security or information security or privacy or risk officer that enters a new company/entity for employment should be taking the first ninety to one hundred twenty days to properly assess the enterprise as a whole, including however many "landscapes" are present, e.g., corporate infrastructure, critical infrastructure, SCADA, e-commerce, supply chain, manufacturing, retail, etc. During this initial phased approach, the new security officer should work in conjunction with a compliance officer and/or governance risk and compliance (GRC) group at your new company. It is possible that either of the two has already conducted an enterprise risk assessment, so it's time to review it closely and identify where your gaps are in the enterprise.

If, for some odd reason, compliance personnel has not conducted one of these in a long time or even over a year, then it's vital, as part of your process, to conduct one yourself. Now that you have decided to conduct one, you will need to choose your base framework and identify if there are any enhancements or additional frameworks to consider. Most companies over the last ten years have been moving away from a handful of frameworks and concentrating on NIST (National Institute of Standards and Technology) and NIST CSF (cybersecurity framework). NIST also has additional enhancements that can be added on to your base framework of NIST or NIST CSF, things like manufacturing (MEP) industry where one of the most important aspects of MEP is to ensure safety among manufacturing environments and safety from cyberattacks and threats that could raise an organization's level of risk by introducing loss-of-life scenarios, which no one wants any part of. In addition to NIST's various enhancements, an organization needs to consider if there are any additional regulatory, compliance, and/or contractual requirements to include as part of your overall risk assessment. Some of these enhancements that might apply are

1. PCI-DSS - Payment Card Industry-Data Security Standard. https://www.pcisecuritystandards.org/documents/PCI%20 SSC%20Quick%20Reference%20Guide.pdf
2. HIPAA - Health Insurance Portability and Accountability Act. https://www.hhs.gov/hipaa/index.html
3. HITRUST - Health Information Trust Alliance. https://hitrustalliance.net/
4. FFIEC - Federal Financial Industry Examination Council. https://www.ffiec.gov/
5. GLBA - Gramm-Leach Bliley Act. https://www.ftc.gov/tips-advice/business-center/privacy-and-security/gramm-leach-bliley-act
6. FDA - Food and Drug Administration. https://www.fda.gov/
7. GDPR - General Data Protection Regulation. https://eugdpr.org/

The list goes on.

Once you have established your base framework and identified any additional controls your organization requires (harmonized approach), it's time to conduct your assessment.

Another aspect of a risk assessment might be an assessment targeting the security architecture of the organization and all its components across the enterprise, typically tools and technology in use across your organization. Sometimes a company might have too much technology that they rely on to stop cyberattacks or too many repeat tools that perform the same work. A targeted security architecture assessment (TSAA) helps an organization with some key deliverables and benefits:

1. The TSAA also utilizes your identified and in use framework for your entity. This ensures that any additional assessments are in line with your previous risk assessments and utilizing the same security controls.

2. Someone from your team, preferable a security architect, will send questions to targeted list of individuals and stakeholders within your company that has specific knowledge of your environments and architecture.

3. The ability to identify "current state" versus "future state" and the information gathered and assessed in your TSAA can help build you three- to five-year roadmap for your security program.

4. Identify and realize a full picture of your tools, applications, hardware, appliances, and other technology within your environments, the owners of each subjected tool, and its use. Eliminate certain tools at EOL (end of life) or even older versions of unsupported operating systems, etc.

5. Identify gaps in people, process, and technology as it relates to your enterprise matched against your framework security controls. Understand your path to remediation for gaps.

6. Help deciding leaders prioritize new security initiatives and overall planning for improving security posture and maturity.

Speaking of maturity, there are assessments that can be utilized to measure the effectiveness of a security program and/or the overall maturity of the security program. In many cases, security operations management tends to conduct maturity assessments of their SOCs, security operation centers, and/or the effectiveness of their SOC operations. In many cases, entities that choose to build an internal SOC team could face challenges with staff shortages, especially within the cyber security industry or even less experienced team members that haven't fully developed their skills, which decreases the overall maturity of the program.

All in all, a risk assessment is important because it will measure your level of risk; identify gaps in your security program, compliance, and posture; help build risk treatment plans and ways to track risks in the organization (risk register). Your company plays a part in understanding what level of risk is acceptable to the organization and who in your organization will own risk? Is it a centralized group, like risk management, or have the executives decided that each business stakeholder will be responsible? These are questions to be asked, thought about, and decided on.

In some cases, and depending on incidents that have or may have occurred at your company, especially related to corporate espionage, cyberattacks, theft of trade secrets, and the list goes on, there are key partnerships that you should have and maintain—your risk management group and your internal audit group. Both groups typically have straight-on connections to the coveted audit committee and/or the board of directors. If you are having difficulty in resolving issues, closing incidents, influencing others, then get on board with these fine folks and find ways to close the issues together.

Chapter 10

Gone to Work for the Competitor

This particular case was one of the biggest and yet complicated cases I worked on involving an insider threat. This case started out as a workplace violence/threatening employee investigation that involved a female employee and a male supervisor. The supervisor was new to the company, and the employee was a long-standing, twenty-plus-years employee. The employee worked out of a store location within the finance department, whereas the supervisor was located in a multistory office building seven miles away. In my initial meeting with HR and the supervisor, they detailed a two-year disagreement with the employee in question and the threat the employee had made more recently that she was going to file a lawsuit against the supervisor and the company. I proceeded to interview the employee's coworkers to try and identify corroborating information related to the employee's story and did not identify any consistent story that was similar to the complaining employee. On the other hand, most of the coworkers described the complaining employee as a strange, moody, and suspicious. This was reported as happening over the last several weeks.

My client, the head of investigations, called me to get my take on the case, from the recent discussions he had me do with the HR and supervisor. Since legal action was mentioned, I reached out to the client's litigation department to inquire on whether any action had, in fact, been filed, and at the time, none were found. HR and the supervisor were determining whether they were going to place the employee on administrative leave or suspension based on her behavior at work. While that determination was underway, I began conducting an internal investigation into the employee and their "behavior and activity" while at work, which included review of e-mails, web and proxy traffic, remote forensic investigation, and other proprietary methods (in-house tools and programs) so that a determination could be made on whether there was another reason for the way the employee was behaving at work.

Typically, in an internal investigation, I would meet with the employee to gather information, but based on the behavior displayed at work and other employee accounts, I chose to wait for the interview once I had a chance to conduct a background. Also, since this investigation began as a workplace violence case, I performed some initial risk assessments on the employee. Initial web traffic and such didn't really indicate anything suspicious or made it necessary to look into further. Although when I conducted the preliminary network forensics (connecting to employee's machine over corporate network), I did see some troubling activity related to excessive printing of documents for numerous days and, in some cases, erratic times. Some of the printer metadata that I was able to glean at was suspicious as some of the naming conventions of the documents could have been indications of employee data.

I reviewed the initial findings of the investigation with my client, as we often did for case review, especially when there was possible criminal statutes in play, and ensured the correct laws violated were identified before moving forward with additional work. At this point, there was enough "probable cause" to continue to the next stage of the investigation. Since initial forensic findings indicated some suspicious behavior, it was necessary to undertake a "black bag" investigation in the middle of the night. In this sense, the goal was to get into the office building where the target employee worked, forensically copy her hard drive for further forensic investigation, and have a search of her work area for any additional information related to the suspicious activity. I had to coordinate my late-night visit with the office manager and so had a discussion with the area vice president as this was a sensitive matter, and he was very supportive of the investigation. I flew to the region where the office was located to meet with the office manager and to enter the building. I was given a key to the building for my visit as well. The office manager informed me that the office cleaners were already done, so no other individuals should be entering the office until 8:00 AM. I needed to figure out a few things, namely how the employee was disposing of or moving the large amount of paper that she had been printing out for some many days. Her coworker had also reported the same information and consistent with her manager; witnessing the employee holding or carrying reams of printouts.

The most important task for me to start was to make that hard drive copy, so at least I had what I originally came for. The copying of the hard drive can take some time, depending on the size of the hard drive, and in her case, the hard drive was quite voluminous and would take at least eight hours to copy. I had arrived at the office at 10:00 PM, so I figured I had plenty of time. As my field computer system used for forensic imaging started up and was on its way in making that copy (I always followed industry best practices and guidelines on seizures and chain of custody), I decided to take a look around the office and determine if there were any hiding spots. I first walked around the floor and closed the blinds in the office, in case there were any outside prying eyes. The office was two levels and also contained an underground garage for employees. The parking garage was protected by a gate, which required a code or remote control to open it. After walking around and not really identifying any areas where objects could be hidden, I walked back to the employee's desk area and performed a search. In one of the desk drawers was a file folder labeled with a rival company's name on it, and the inside file contained an offer letter and employment contract with the employee's apparent signatures and acceptance of new employment. I made photocopies of both documents and put the file back where I had found it. In one of the employee's bottom drawers was what appeared to be some printouts of customer contact details, including highly-sensitive information, including PII (personally identifiable information), Social Security number's, driver's license information, and in some cases, passport numbers and bank account information. In some states, possession of this data in this format is considered a felony in itself. I also photographed this information for evidence and placed it back in the drawer. During my search, I also encountered a second laptop. According to corporate IT records, the employee only had one laptop assigned. I documented the identification numbers of the laptop and then photographed the sides, front and back, of the laptop for evidence.

By now, surprisingly, the forensic copy was completed in only six hours, so I was relieved at this. I started to close up the gear when I noticed headlights from a car circling the office building several times. I ended up looking for a place to peer through without being noticed and identified a late model car with a female driver. Then I heard the garage gate start to clank open and now wondering who this individual was entering the garage at 3:00 a.m. I was able to get near the back of the garage in a maintenance area where I would be conspicuous and be able to view the garage area. Luckily, the client had CCTV cameras at multiple vantage spots in the garage, so anything I might have missed visually would likely be picked up by CCTV. The vehicle entered the parking lot and the driver pulled head into a parking spot and then deliberately began in reverse and backed the car close to the rear of the garage next to oil barrels and the trash dumpster. The employee then opened their trunk and proceeded to move some crates around so she could step into the trash dumpster and retrieve the reams of paper she apparently printed out. From the looks of it, there was clearly enough paper to fit fifty to sixty reams of paper. Then the employee stepped out of the dumpster and opened the oil barrels that were standing next to the trash dumpster. Again, the employee continued to empty the barrels by picking up reams of paper that were clearly printed with black printer ink. All in all, it appeared as if the employee had taken or removed in excess of 180 reams worth of paper and placed them in the trunk of her car. The employee returned to the driver's seat and proceeded to open the garage gate by remote control and exited the garage area. The employee did not return to the office until her shift began at 9:00 AM. I contacted the client's physical security monitoring center and requested the images from the garage CCTV for the last twenty-four hours and to maintain chain of custody and that I would pick them up in a few hours.

The activity witnessed in the middle of the night, coupled with the evidence identified in the employee's desk area, initial forensic investigation, and now completed hard drive forensic investigation, identified concretely the activity perpetrated by the target employee. I contacted a local prosecutor to determine if they would be interested in prosecuting the case, and because of our long running partnership and clear evidence of criminality, the prosecutor agreed to prosecute.

Next, it was time to conduct an interview of the employee for the purposes of garnering admission and/or written confession of her activity. The interview extended for four hours, with time to grant breaks for the employee when requested. The employee began responding in the defensive and then slowly became combative and then refused to answer any questions without her attorney present. I quickly reminded the employee that this was a corporate investigation and that she did not have the right to an attorney for these purposes (and this was not a de facto law enforcement interview with Miranda reading), and if she, in fact, wanted to cease the interview, then HR would be notified of her actions. The employee then agreed to continue on with the interview and finally succumbed to the truth and provided a written confession of her activity over the last three weeks.

CHAPTER 10
Case in Review and Recommendations

The forensic investigation clearly delineated the activity performed by the employee that consisted of several weeks of performing database searches for client-specific information and the printing of the data to her local office printer near her desk area. Evidence also indicated the storage of trade secrets and confidential information saved to external hard drives and USB thumb drives and the forwarding of work-related e-mails to several personal e-mail accounts over a three-week period. The second laptop identified during the search of the employee's desk was determined to be an original laptop assigned to the employee over twenty years previous and was never returned to IT when her new laptop was issued. During the interview and proceeding the written confession, the employee was informed that she would be placed on suspension until the case was completed.

Recommendations:

1. Computer System Logging - In certain highly-regulated industries, maintaining some form of auditing of keystrokes is highly recommended. Example, not related to this investigation, the banking industry often maintains keystroke logging for banker systems performing transactions. Additional logging and security monitoring is important for a mature cyber security posture and resilience standpoint.

2. USB and Computer Ports - Some clients make the decision to enforce a policy that restricts the use of USB and external hard drives, especially in companies that deal with highly-sensitive data, trade secrets, and confidential information. In some cases, exceptions can be made as business need warrants, but monitoring for compliance is strongly suggested.

3. Corporate Security Partnership - It was always the case of corporate security leadership building relationships with other business leaders. In this case, several employees witnessed the target employee acting suspicious, including the carrying of reams of paper, but did not know who to report this activity to. Educating employees with security awareness information and reporting guidelines are important so that all incidents are reported in a timely manner.

4. Data Loss Prevention (DLP) - If the company had deployed DLP for e-mail at the employee endpoints, then when the employee sent work e-mails containing sensitive information, DLP rules would have quarantined the e-mails for further review and could have indicated suspicious activity on the part of the employee and triggered the investigation.

5. Manager Review of Office Areas - Oftentimes corporate policy might dictate that managers are responsible for checking desk and work areas to ensure no sensitive data has been left out in the open. This company had a policy similar to it but appended the policy for offices similar to this one, that garage space, dumpsters, and other containers in the garage and around the office were also checked before locking up for the night to prevent similar investigations.

Chapter 11

Shared Service Third-Party Privacy Nightmare

I was consulted by a client of mine—a chief security officer of a global consumer-products organization. The company, as a whole, had made a management decision to outsource much of their IT, human resources, and finance and supply chain to a third-party "shared service" provider. I was engaged in this issue because my client needed some assistance in educating the shared service provider on proper security and privacy concepts, as well assist him with overseeing some of the projects and initiatives from various business units, essentially a consulting gig with some professional service hours. In this context, consulting soon led to investigation and incident response because of some of the shared service employees.

Over the next few weeks, I met with numerous leads and managers from the shared service provider to understand their level of understanding on security and privacy, and then based on their level of understanding, I would then modify my delivery. Unfortunately, most of the people I spoke to were "green" in knowledge of proper industry-level security and privacy concepts, let alone compliance requirements around data privacy, GDPR, and other regulations. I informed my client of the challenge he was going to have with not only the number of shared service contractors that were working onsite at company facilities, but also the remote offices where help desk and back office HR and finance operations were taking place.

The shared service company claimed to have on staff the appropriate levels of security and privacy management, industry-appropriate certifications, company policy and process for security and privacy, etc., but soon enough, it was known that this company was far from where they claimed to be.

About a month into the consulting project, my client asked if I could partner with his contact in legal office that was working on a project with the shared service company involving the storage, collection, and use of employee PII (personal identifiable information), PHI (protected health information), and other sensitive data on a global basis. The initial issue was the application in use for this project was based in an Eastern European country. There were no protections in place, especially for GDPR, let alone standard data privacy requirements to protect the data in play. The shared service provider did not want to encrypt the data in transit nor at rest, claiming the change would be too costly. Conversations went round and round for weeks on end until the third party finally agreed to make the necessary changes. They also made an agreement to ensure GDPR country data was not leaving borders for other countries as well. Needless to say, as the application was in the build phase, test phase, and then finally production, the process continued to start utilizing this new application for all employee records and documents. About three weeks into production, the CSO received a call from another company claiming that his company (client) employee records were being e-mailed to this other company, and much of the information was quite sensitive. I was again engaged by the client to initiate their incident response protocol and dig into the incident to determine how this event occurred.

Having been involved in the prior project with the application in question and after reviewing the e-mails sent (disclosed) to the other company, metadata suggested that the e-mails did, in fact, originate from the shared service application based primarily on the e-mail header information. I reached out to the application owner to inform him what was occurring and to shut down the e-mail service immediately. As a matter of fact, all those weeks of reviewing the project, never once did this guy mention e-mail service or process, and why would there need to be an SMTP (simple mail transfer protocol)-style service in place for handling of records? It was determined after speaking to the application owner that he developed a process (internal) for all records newly created in the system; an e-mail would be sent to an administrator informing them of the new record. The e-mail, unfortunately, contained some sensitive information about the employees. I had the application owner review his process and the e-mail address where the e-mails would be sent to determine what had happened. Sure enough, the application owner indicated that when the developer had entered the target e-mail address, it was entered incorrectly, thus disclosing employee data to an unauthorized third party.

I notified the client to inform him of the outcome of the investigation and the apparent mistake by the application owner who was able to successfully modify the information to reflect the proper contact. It was also determined that while there was no malintent by the third-party shared service employee, the activity fit into the category I liked to use—negligent insider. This is a person—an employee, vendor, or contractor—that could be lazy, tired, doesn't follow policy, etc., that while performing an activity like code development, causes a security incident; they are negligent in their actions.

Case in Review and Recommendations

More and more companies are outsourcing various parts of their business to third-party shared service companies. Looking back ten to fifteen years, companies would primarily utilize shared service organizations to augment IT responsibilities, help desk and support functions, to name a few. Some banks and financial institutions called on shared service organizations for outbound sales support and would utilize offshore companies to maintain cost savings.

Recommendations:

1. Security departments, managers, and leaders should be part of the solution, not the problem, in any organization. If the company is in the process of making decisions to utilize any third party, this fits into the scheme of third-party risk and, therefore, should be properly assessed until completed and approved by the CISO and/or highest information security leader.

2. Mergers and Acquisitions (M&A) - If your company is thinking of merging with or acquiring another entity, a proper risk assessment is necessary. This could include questionnaires and review of the entity's information security policies, incident response plans, and last SOC2 or other similar report, looking for any exceptions noted by the auditor.

3. Information Security Policy - Having internal discussions early with appropriate stakeholders on the responsibility of contractor companies, especially shared service companies, as their name implies, they have multiple clients that they provide service to, and they need to be assured that information and data are kept safe, secure, and completely separate from other entities. The same thing applies to any requirement you make of your

own employees; all contractors and third parties should also maintain the same requirements. These are all decisions that should be made early on and not during a security incident because your third party couldn't spell "security."

4. Auditing of Shared Service Locations - Ensure that your contracts include the right to audit and/or visit locations at any time (or coordinated time, etc.) to ensure they are in full compliance with your requirements. There also should be the requirement that they will provide full access to appropriate staff members and other identified individuals when requested or warranted.

5. Client Reviews - You will most certainly want to talk with a number of their customer references so that you can understand the complete picture, any challenges, pain points, etc. Have the ability to speak to your peer at the references too.

Chapter 12

Counterfeits

At some point in our lives, we have come across someone selling those flashy DVDs on the corner, the subway, on the train, and down in the underground parking lot. For some, they sell a few merchandise that they may have picked up from another person or at a flea market, and usually, the quality is pretty crappy. For the large percentage of these DVD hustlers, they are part of an organized crime ring, with access to high availability duplication equipment that offers some of the best quality around, almost as if the movie was taken right off the production line.

This investigation was a multi-part one. The beginning of it, I was working undercover for an industry organization fighting the prevalence of movie counterfeits. Various industry offices around the world would carry out long extensive investigations, undercover buys, and in some cases, surveillance investigations; most times working with law enforcement agencies to ensure quick arrests; and in some cases, "pocket subpoena" power to raid illegal storefronts, warehouses, and unauthorized distribution channels.

The second part of the investigation identified insiders working in film-duplication labs, unbeknownst to the labs that these insiders were part of this particular organized crime ring.

Most of these investigations began with reviewing advertisements on classified sites, scouring the hundreds of ads looking for the right ones. Sometimes we struck out, but many times we hit the lottery. In a small number of cases, such as this one, we hit the motherlode because of the size and complexity of the players involved and, in some cases, the many facets of counterfeits that were in play by the bad actors. We identify the right ad usually because the seller is identifying movies that have yet to be released in the movie theaters (globally). On this particular day, we identified an individual selling a number of non-released movie titles. I began communicating with the individual over e-mail, utilizing an authorized undercover account (had been identified and approved by law enforcement) to try and set up a meet-up time and location to check out the merchandise.

The individual (target) responded rather quickly. My back story was that I was a large actor in the area with strong distribution channels and a team of street sellers under my belt. I needed regular distribution as I could sell high quantity weekly. The target was quite interested in the offer and asked if I had cash available, which I responded that I did have cash for transactions. We agreed to meet up at a local supermarket underground parking lot. An hour later, my team and I (investigation) were set up in the parking lot with full surveillance. The target arrived as promised, and we met up. I brought with me a portable DVD player so that I could review the merchandise. Upon review, it was found that the quality of the DVD was professional, and the content was from a master copy, which could mean the target had contact with an industry insider. This would be determined later. I asked the target if I could purchase all of his inventory on hand for $5,000. He agreed. I told him I'd like to review and then probably set up a later time in the next week to get together and discuss a formal deal. The target was in agreement. I had my surveillance team continue to follow the target and gather any additional demographics on him. The surveillance team reported back that the target appeared to be careful in his movements when he departed the meet-up location, and to not spook him, they decided it was best to split the surveillance.

After returning to the office, I reviewed all the materials purchased, and all were similar in that they were all duplicated from a master copy. Most master copies include some sort of watermarking identification that is sometimes visible and not visible. We sent off one of the copies for forensic review to try and identify the matter's origin to then track the location of duplication facilities.

About three days later, I reached back out to the target by undercover e-mail to attempt another meet up over coffee to discuss physical distribution plans and ordering strategy. The target responded rather quickly, and we agreed to another meet-up. The target wanted me to pick a location. I chose a location that was very public (to try and appease the target's apparent concerns of being watched) but still a location that had been used in the past and some good vantage points for surveillance operations.

We met up a couple of days later at the agreed upon spot. My surveillance team was in place in a variety of vantage spots to ensure we captured accurate intelligence, including the actual meet up. My video surveillance guy was a friend of mine that worked at the local law enforcement, doing the same thing but moonlighting on the side. So I had top-notch guys and gals working. The target showed up but this time with an additional individual, which was unannounced. I questioned the additional person, and the target mentioned that he was his security guy and he felt he needed the additional support. I commented that next time, please mention it earlier, instead of surprising me. I had to stay in character, e.g., supposed to be a one-on-one meeting but now there is this additional individual. The target apologized for his lapse in judgment. We continued, and I started to describe my "operation" that included thirty street sellers positioned across the city and that I figured I would need five hundred DVDs per month to start and review after a couple of months on whether I need to increase the quantity. The target wanted $15 per DVD—$7,500 per month. I rebutted, and we agreed upon $10 per DVD—$5,000 per month for now. The target asked when I wanted to start, and I asked the target when he thought he could have five hundred DVDs ready. The target thought about it, talked to his security person, and then said he could have it within a week. I agreed with the schedule, and we set up a time and place to meet so that we could exchange money and merchandise weekly. Essentially, Fridays were the days, and the target told me he would get back to me with a place and time that worked. We departed.

About two days later, out of the blue, the target sent me an e-mail asking if I was interested in having a deeper discussion at his operation location, a.k.a. his house. I thought it was interesting that the target was moving this quickly with feeling comfortable in having me know where he lives, but I figured it was mostly greed on his part. He was looking at $5,000 a month and more for what was easy for him to duplicate copies and such, but maybe there were other intentions. We scheduled a date and time, and he provided me the address, and I said I would see him then. The target commented he was excited to show me more about his business and meet his operation. I shared the same "excitement."

The next question for us was how we were going to handle surveillance. Obviously, we could have exterior teams doing the same as previous, but once I enter the residence, we would be dark. Since we were working/partnering with law enforcement, we had a meeting, and I suggested that since this op was starting to move quicker than expected, I wanted to ensure we had as much intelligence and suggested a wire so we at least had audio and possibly video as well. It was agreed, and I was fit for invisible devices to avoid detection.

I headed out to the target's location, all surveillance teams were set up, as well as a QRF (quick reaction force), should that aspect be necessary. The target lived in a hilly section of the city and mostly residential with single family homes. There were a couple of late to recent vehicles parked in the driveway. I walked up and rang the bell, and the target answered the door, and I went inside. We walked into a large living room space, had some views out the back windows. There were some very old pieces of furniture. There was a female sitting on the sofa, watching TV (later identified as target's girlfriend), and the security guy I had met previously was also sitting in the living room. We both sat down in the living room to have our discussion. The target started by saying that he was excited about the new relationship and was hoping to expand on the business we were conducting now simply because of my "thirty-person street team." The target was obviously greedy, so why not capitalize on that? We talked further, and he wanted to give me a tour of his duplication facility, located on the north side of his home. There appeared to be three bedrooms that the target had knocked down so he could have an open concept on this wing of the home. There were multiple duplication stations situated around this large area, along with printing and design services for custom DVD cover artwork and additional artwork as required by customers. An area was also set aside for shipping/logistics, and according to the target, some of his buyers were out of state, so shipping was necessary. There were four people working the various stations, and the target commented that he could increase the number of staff depending on customer demand. We then left the duplication area and walked back into the living room. The target wanted to discuss our future working together. The target took me into another room, his bedroom, where he customized a floor-to-ceiling vault in what used to be his walk-in closet. The target started to say that this was the side of the business he wanted to work with me on. He opened the vault, and inside were piles of other counterfeit merchandise—watches, bags, leather goods, T-shirts, clothing—and then there was his money (cash) stash, and by the looks of it, it's about $1 million (ten bricks of $100,000). The target also had weapons inside the vault that he said were for protection, and he apologized for not warning me. I commented it was okay. I told the target I was definitely interested in this part of the business as he seemed to be very successful. I commented that we should discuss at another time as it was getting late and I had another meeting to attend to. I departed and left the area, with surveillance in tow.

The team met back at the law enforcement office to discuss the meet-up with the target and to discuss the next steps for the case. At this point, the visit to the target's home revealed much information about the operation, capabilities, and other facets, including the cash and weapons. We decided to continue buying the merchandise for the next couple of weeks and to hold a meeting to discuss the additional counterfeit merchandise. I reached out to the target to schedule the next buy, which he accepted, and he asked me to come to his home at the end of the week to make the exchange as he told me he trusted me. That Friday and that next Friday, the buys and exchanges of money for merchandise went as planned. During the second exchange, the target asked if I had time to think about his proposition, and I confirmed that I did and was ready when he was. As I was at his home, we had a discussion about the counterfeit items, and I mentioned that I had received lots of interest from at least ten of my street sellers, and the requests were typically leather goods, including handbags. The top brands of interest to people were always the luxury goods retailers, to which the target commented that those were the types of bags the target could sell. He asked how many bags I would need for the first order. I told the target that we could start with two bags per brand times ten street sellers, so forty bags altogether, and I could test the market. I asked what the per-piece price would be, and he mentioned he wanted $1,200 per piece—$48,000. I told the target I would discuss with my team, as that was a lot of money, and I would get back to him. I left and had a call with law enforcement team to discuss the new ask for $48,000 for the other counterfeit pieces. The interesting point on these pieces were that when I originally saw them in the vault, they looked very close to being real merchandise; that is how well they were. I reached out to the target by e-mail to ask some questions regarding the bags. I was trying to determine his source for these bags and to figure what sort of quantities he had access to. I asked very open-ended questions to try and garner his greed behavior and gather additional information. The target responded after a few hours and went into great detail that he had an insider contact at one of the fashion houses that supplied real merchandise to the counterfeiter outfit that would duplicate the items, and then they would sell them through store fronts controlled by gangs in and around Chinatown area and through individuals like our target. The fashion insider was also a gang member that had infiltrated the fashion house for some time in an operations capacity. (See the next chapter that discusses that portion of the case.) The target confirmed that he had high quantities if needed, and you could hear his greed coming through his writing. I said that I would be in touch but that I wanted to proceed with the first order for forty bags at $48,000 but requested a discount since I was planning for a rather large order. The target and I discussed, and he was happy to discount it to $25,000. I told the target I would have cash in two days and we could meet up for the exchange.

The target called a day later and asked if we could hold the exchange a day earlier, and I commented that I could indeed meet early. The plan was to conduct a raid once the exchange was made with the target. I was once again outfitted with an audio and video wire with a duffel of $48,000 in small bills as requested by the target. The plan was to have me enter the home first, wait five minutes, and then have teams conduct raid with no-knock warrant. At this point, the team had widened with multiple agencies involved as there was a host of criminal violations in clear sight, and everyone worked well together. The other part of the plan was to "arrest" me along with the target and accomplices to preserve my identity. I arrived at the target's location, knocked on the door, and entered as I had in the past. The security guy was present and asked for the cash so he could verify the amount. I handed over the cash. The target went into his bedroom and later returned with the forty bags as we discussed. As the target and I were having a discussion, the police arrived and raided the premises. I, along with the target, his security, girlfriend, and workers, were arrested and read Miranda. A transport van was outside awaiting all prisoners to be taken to city jail for processing.

All members were interviewed and interrogated once processed. The girlfriend who always appeared to be unaffiliated with the target's business was actually aware of the business and operations. The girlfriend was crying during the interview as she was just finishing high school and had plans to attend college in the fall. This aspect was utilized by investigators to "turn" the girlfriend and find out as much as possible about the operation, including the most important aspect—the contact that was supplying high-quality master copies. After all, this was the insider we were always targeting, but in these types of investigations, there will likely be middlemen and other accomplices that get caught up. The girlfriend was a minor at the time, and her parents were contacted to come into the police station. The parents also wanted their daughter to cooperate. The girlfriend was hesitant to start but then decided to cooperate in exchange for full immunity as prosecutors agreed to grant immunity for her information, cooperation, and testimony if the case went to trial phase. The girlfriend was able to identify the duplication company and insider that was friends with the target. The girlfriend turned over e-mails and other evidence to prove the relationship, the exchange of money transactions, and other communications that would ensure the case would be solid. The case progressed following my involvement with the insider arrested and prosecuted, along with the target, both receiving multiyear prison terms.

CHAPTER 12
Case in Review and Recommendations

This case and investigation were certainly specialized and uncommon for most corporate investigators, but certainly for professionals working in the anti-counterfeiting area, this story is probably very familiar. There was a period when I worked on several of these style investigations/cases and field raids on store fronts and kiosks involved in the selling of counterfeit products throughout the Americas. There are no real recommendations to provide here since this was outside-the-box investigation. The film distributor did everything right and had all protections in place, which assisted investigators in tracking down the origin of the master copies and having the ability to know this important part, as an interview with the target may have revealed the information we were after.

Suggestions:

1. In times of delivering master copies to third-party vendors, use secure methods, such as courier services (well vetted and approved, bonded, insured, etc.) that will track shipments and cover chain of custody at all points of compromise.
2. During preview events at movie theaters, film companies/distributors should maintain chain of custody through the process, as well as provide armed security services at theaters while the masters/copies are in movie theater hands.
3. In connection to the above, provide and/or hire specialized third-party services to monitor film preview events for unauthorized filming of movie content, along with established protocol to partner with law enforcement or theater security to enforce arrests, seizure, and removal of individuals.

Chapter 13

Luxury Counterfeits

It was coincidental that this case connected to the previous case/ investigation, so I figured I would include the case in this book as just another example of how a malicious insider played a part to circumvent security controls to carry out their activity. The world of luxury brand counterfeits is prevalent across the world and, in some countries, permissible to a degree, e.g., in some Asian countries, there are controlled buying centers—an entire area set up with kiosks and store fronts of sellers offering their counterfeit watches, bracelets, clothing, bags, purses, trunks, shoes, games, etc. In some Chinatown settings within US cities, counterfeit operations have also come and go, typically business taking place in the back rooms and basements within legal store front locations, buyers needing to know the correct name of the person to request for, or in some cases, a certain gesture toward the sellers so they know your reason for shopping in their store.

Information gathered from the girlfriend of the target in the last case provided some context to the luxury brand insider as well as the specific store fronts utilized for merchandise pick-ups in Chinatown and their associated contacts. I had made contact with the luxury brand counterfeit investigation office, someone I met just weeks ago at an industry training session held with law enforcement in a joint meeting, learning how to identify counterfeits for various brands under the brand umbrella. I explained the case and information identified so far and wanted to gain the brand's interest in a formal investigation into the matter at hand. The brand was also going to conduct their own internal (in tandem) investigation since the target included an insider that was likely gang-affiliated working at the luxury brand offices. We got the green light to move forward with the investigation.

The team gathered to review a plan for the investigation. Surveillance was going to be vital to this case as usual, so some extra planning was necessary to identify best vantage points and such. Since we already gathered some store front locations, as well as the luxury retailer location where the insider worked, we could implement round-the-clock surveillance of the insider. Typically, in these sorts of investigations, there could be multiple points of contact (subjects) and locations utilized as part of the scheme, so we decided to run a seventy-two-hour surveillance operation against the insider first to gather normal routines, individuals of contact, locations, and other demographics.

As that surveillance was happening, we sent in female investigators as shoppers to some of the store front locations that were identified from the girlfriend (last case) to determine if the buying operations were still alive and whether the investigators could make some purchases. Sure enough, many of the store front locations were still in operating mode of selling counterfeit luxury accessories and leather goods. In one instance, a female investigator noted in her report that after she entered the store location, a woman approached her and asked if she could assist her. At that time, the female investigator looked around the shop and said she didn't really see anything that caught her eye but commented on the luxury goods retailer photo sitting in the store's front window, so she inquired about what that meant. The woman walked away for a second and then returned, according to the report, and then escorted the investigator into a back room, closed the door, and started to discuss additional merchandise that was available for sale. The woman pulled out a binder for the investigator to flip through, picking out items she was interested in. The investigator identified three different bags that she liked and asked the woman if they were available. At that time, the woman said they were. The woman told the investigator the prices, and the investigator agreed and paid for the merchandise. The woman wrapped up the merchandise, and the sale was completed. The merchandise was taken back to the office for examination and confirmation of its status as counterfeit. The merchandise was documented by taking photographs, assigned evidence numbers (bagged and tagged), and stored for later use.

The surveillance team that was tailing the target also reported back around the same time, detailing at great lengths the individuals and locations that the target visited with. We repeated surveillance on the target for the full seventy-two hours, which was a good amount of time to figure out the target's pattern. In some cases I worked in the past, surveillance between seventy-two and ninety hours was usually sufficient time to piece together the target's pattern of activity. This target, however, appeared to be tied down to only a few movements before showing up for work and after he left work. The target's details from surveillance was handed over to our investigations team to further enumerate the individuals and the locations visited. The investigations team was able to identify some of the individuals met by the target as members of well-known gangs based on our own records and of law enforcement contacts in the area. Further enumeration of the store fronts where counterfeit merchandise was sold were all owned by an LLC that was later determined to be owned by a Chinese multinational company known for illegal business dealings globally. There was some indication that local gang members were part of this business based on information that was identified after several dumpster dives for trash/documents and other evidence. During the surveillance, there was a location that was visited by the target that was determined to be a warehouse in Chinatown. Additional surveillance was conducted on the warehouse at varying times of the day and evening to determine if this warehouse was "live," meaning were there shipments and trucks delivering merchandise and other goods on a regular basis, as this location could be the central point of the investigation and where all the goods could be located. In fact, further surveillance did show various shipping containers and trucks that would deliver on a regular basis. Through identification of shipping trucks and containers, further investigation could identify the origin of the goods that were being delivered.

A meeting took place between the luxury goods representatives and law enforcement to decide on a plan on moving forward. At this point, we had sufficient evidence of organized crime, and the hope was that further search warrants would yield great results. Law enforcement was able to obtain search warrants on the three store front locations, the target's residence, and the warehouse previously identified. The plan was for simultaneous early-morning raids to avoid people not being present at the locations. The result was successful as the store fronts had merchandise, along with sales receipts and other documentation, that could prove there was a selling operation in existence and other documents identifying managing partners and individuals of interest out of Asia. The warehouse was also filled with merchandise and associated paperwork, documents, and other evidence that were important to the case. The target's residence had a stash of legitimate goods, along with other counterfeit goods, including DVDs from the previous case (previous chapter) and cash along with the weapons, that were apparently taken from the store location.

Case in Review and Recommendations

This case is very similar to chapter 12 in that if you, the professional, are employed in loss prevention and/or brand protection/counterfeit investigations, then these scenarios would be very familiar to you. As highlighted in this chapter, there was a crossover from the other counterfeit case that bled into this case, so opportune to highlight both cases. This case is significantly tied to Asian gang activity and similar to other counterfeit cases and trends with luxury retailer brands and unauthorized selling channels. The interesting aspect with any organized crime group or gang is there is likely to be tertiary activity and criminal violations that could help in building/developing a much stronger case. In some aspects with previous investigations of this nature (counterfeits) and its familial match with piracy cases, the investigation could lead to a stronger component of Racketeer Influenced and Corrupt Act (RICO) and harsher financial crime violations leading to stiffer penalties, restitution, and federal sentencing guidelines.

Recommendations:

1. Retailers should spend time educating their employees on how to identify counterfeit products in an effort to decrease chances that bad actors will attempt to return the counterfeit merchandise in exchange for a credit to be used on legitimate merchandise. Ensure that your assets (people) at the front lines are well trained and receive regular awareness of new trends so that they can assist and stop counterfeit activity early.

2. Always ensure that local offices adhere to corporate guidelines on background checks for all employees; in this case, the insider was hired in an operations role where the employee would not be handling monetary transactions, and therefore, the company management at the local level made the decision not to conduct

a full background since the employee was hired on a temporary basis, for the holidays, and was apparently a friend of another full-time employee.

3. Security measures within back rooms and operational areas should always have measures and controls in place to prevent and deter criminal activity. In this case, it was determined that loss prevention was not present at all times because of staff shortages, and the bags and boxes were not checked prior to exiting the store premises through backdoors.

4. Partner with Local Law Enforcement - We all have those gut feelings. If you have a gut feeling on a guy or gal who was just hired, who has multiple Chinese-character tattoos and acts suspiciously around the workplace, and you think the individual might be associated with criminal activity, most law enforcement agencies will allow corporate security departments the ability to report issues and incidents privately (non-public) for follow up.

Chapter 14

Risk Mitigation Strategies

There have been a variety of investigations and cases described within the book, all different in context and situations, except for one common theme; they all were related to a target of the investigation that was identified as an insider. Earlier in the book, I have also described the importance of conducting some form of risk assessment. Risk assessment is an important baseline to understand the current state of affairs for security and risk, measure any gaps that might be in existence, measure against security controls within a certain framework that leads to the creation of a formalized risk treatment plan and risk register to keep track of enterprise risks. Newly identified risks and potential threats can be added to the risk register. I have discussed many recommendations for mitigating risk throughout the book, primarily following each case and investigation. This chapter will go into more detail regarding measures that can be adopted to mitigate risk. The best you can do try to incorporate "security by design" concepts into your culture, provide ongoing awareness and education to employees (and leaders too), incorporate in-depth defense concepts with people, process, and technology with the result of making it as difficult as possible for the attacker or bad actor to do harm to your company or organization. Since we tend to assess people, process, and technology, I am dividing up recommendation this way:

People

If you have worked in the industry for some time, then you know that we have a shortage of qualified talent, especially within the cybersecurity industry. People are important part of your mitigation strategy. We need people and teams to perform our jobs and carry out our mission, objectives, and charter. No matter if we are speaking about a cybersecurity team or physical security team or an investigations team, we need enough team members to fight the good fight.

1. If you are a leader just hired or starting a new position at an entity, the risk assessment will be a good start and good use for advocating for budget, tools, and people. Use risk assessment process for everything necessary so that you achieve good footing at the start of your program.
2. Assess the current staffing levels that you have now and determine if additional staff are necessary. Match staff needs to your long-term roadmap strategy as needed. Also assess current staff to determine if they are, in fact, in the right roles and/or if they should be repurposed in another role or even a new group.
3. Write roles and responsibilities for each role within your team. This is important on many fronts and required in some cases with compliance and framework controls. You can utilize job descriptions as part of the role and responsibilities. It is important that each person on the team is clear about what their role entails and what their responsibilities are.
4. Job Descriptions for Hiring Qualified Candidates - Use your intuition when hiring new talent for your open roles. I have seen some leaders are very black and white when it comes to a certain job. As an example, a security analyst most definitely should have a core competency with security monitoring, understanding threats, etc. With the job market the way it is today, and many students grabbing their masters in cybersecurity, now they think they are ready to jump in and get a job. The issue is this newly graduated individual has no real-world experience, and for them

to gain experience, they need hands-on type work, and many of these individuals will target the security analyst position. Be careful in hiring—don't just hire bodies because you need them. Hire people that have that requisite experience and skills. Those changing industries and getting an education should be asking companies if there are internships available—this is a better way for them to garner and learn the skills they will need. The same goes for a threat-hunter position. In the past, I have hired threat hunters that had a basic understanding of cyber security but had extensive experience as an investigator. We all know, especially investigators, that you can't teach someone without investigation experience how to investigate and conduct investigations. Sometimes going out on a limb and thinking outside the box is a good approach, if it makes sense.

5. Training - Everyone should have ongoing training and educational opportunities, could be a conference or possibly an educational class in a subject that is relevant to the workplace or the job. It is important to fight for your employees and establish the requirements from your manager that your employees should receive a certain amount of training per year. After all, it's your budget, and you should be able to manage that budget. Your way, your rules. There should also be parameters around education and training to ensure that employees are not taking advantage and partying the entire time, instead of actually learning. Conferences are a great opportunity for employees to not only learn in a class or lab, but also learn about new technology (exhibits) and network with their clients and peers. Conferences could also be a great time for team building— taking the whole team to the conference and doing some team building exercises, programs, and outings to strengthen the team.

Process

This is a great subject that I always like to discuss. Process can also include policy, standards, as well as guidelines. Process is fundamental to any program, not just security or investigations. Most compliance requirements, along with security controls (frameworks), require a certain level of process to be established. So many departments are missing this aspect and should have some level of documentation—at a minimum, an information security policy with standards is a great start. Too often I see companies that have never had a security policy wait and defer before implementing their policies and procedures because then they actually have to start enforcing it, and there is a good chance they might not be ready to.

1. ISMS - Information security management system under ISO 27001 is a framework of policies and procedures that covers various controls to minimize risk as part of an organization's overall risk management strategy.

2. Information Security Policy - An enterprise's overarching policy for addressing concepts and aspects of delivering information security posture to the organization. The information security policy will also include associated standards for all aspects and areas of the policy, e.g., password standard, access standard, security monitoring standard. The standards can also be tied to your organization-specific security controls as mandated through compliance and regulatory requirements.

3. Acceptable Use Policy - Essentially lists out the acceptable and unacceptable uses of the Internet and network resources of an organization. The AUP, as it is also referred to, began in the 1990s as an enforceable policy for Internet service providers (ISPs) and their Internet users as a guide to what activity was okay while using the ISP. The policy was a way for the ISP to enforce violations by users, typically by carrying out activities that ranged from spamming to abuse, fraud, harassment, criminal violations, child exploitation, denial of service attacks,

and other malicious activities. The AUP has been adopted by many organizations, including corporate environments, as another measure in enforcing overall policy at a company.

4. Ethics Policy or Statement - Corporations specially strive to maintain ethical relationships and operations with their clients, employees, and vendors. Many companies will include in their policy toolbelt an ethics policy that covers a lot more than just AUP-style activities but also areas that deal with how vendors are managed, what gifts are acceptable from vendors, how employees are expected to act even participate in corporate investigations, and more importantly, how to report violations of the policy.

5. Incident Response - An incident response plan is vital to ensure that an organization understands the process for responding to an actual and/or alleged security incident, roles and responsibilities, the plan overall, and the necessary steps to achieve an outcome. As part of an Incident Response plan, the company will identify a person that will manage the incident overall. The incident commander that will lead the incident response from beginning to end, including the triage aspect with the front line personnel that reported the incident in the first place and those familiar with the incident. Then briefings with the IR team - usually key stakeholders including CISO, General Counsel, Risk Management, Corporate Communications, etc. Next devising a way forward for investigations and remediation and whether computer forensics is necessary. Do you have a third-party IR firm on retainer? This will be important if you lack internal expertise in this area. It is also a good idea and best practice to conduct ongoing training and tabletop exercises for incident response with varying incident scenarios. In the end, at the completion of handling the incident, the Incident Commander should conduct a root cause analysis, to identify lessons learned during the handling and response to the incident and how to improve moving forward. The root cause analysis should identify whether additional mitigation steps are

necessary, including policy changes, additional processes, hiring additional headcount, etc. Run Books - These would be in relation to your security operations charter and how you monitor security threats and recognize events in your environment. The run books are processes for handling key security events; for example, if your organization experienced a malware infection, what steps are needed to identify the endpoints affected, how to investigate, what tools could be used for the investigation, and then how to remediate the issue. Are there additional personnel necessary to assist with remediation? Also, is this event categorized as a security incident? And if so, what is the process to pull the trigger for incident response? Having clear and concise processes for events that are more likely than not to occur in the environment is a great way to ensure consistent handling by any person that works on the team and ensure everyone is trained on the same information.

6. Roles and Responsibilities - This aspect will come up in many forms and discussions because it's a compliance and regulatory requirement—understanding what each person's role in security is, what their specific responsibilities will be, and how they will be held accountable. In addition to their everyday work and responsibilities, some staff may be part of additional teams, task forces, and response teams, and equally important, they need to understand their specific role and responsibility when it applies to the task at hand. As an example, you might assign a security analyst as a scribe for all security incidents and incident response. The scribe is one of the most important roles during the IR plan because there are so many moving parts and people working in different directions. It is important to document all activities at all times to ensure a proper level of communication. After all, this communication will likely be sent to the executives and board members in some instances.

7. Asset Inventory - A fundamental security rule is to understand your assets—inventory of all assets and a comprehensive list at that, including who owns the asset, who owns the applications

that may run on the asset, and more importantly, what assets are deemed critical. Knowing you critical assets will assist you in your investigations with incident response and business continuity.

Technology

There are many mind-sets when it comes to technology and tools in the environment. Today there are still those organizations that buy and implement tools in their organization but only for compliance reasons, and I like to refer to them as "checkbox for compliance." They may have tools deployed like firewalls and intrusion-detection systems (IDS), but they are not configured to really perform in the way they were designed. On the other side of the spectrum, following the many cyber breaches announced, many companies decided to go spend millions of dollars and buy every piece of technology they could, deploy it in their environment, and hope that they will keep the bad guys out. The problem with this is after a time and not really having a good idea of what tools were in place or what function they were serving, there could be replication of duties, overuse within the network, and an inappropriate strategy for moving forward. Having too many alerts by forty different tools is not going to be sustainable moving forward.

1. Target Security Architecture Assessment - I know I may have included this piece under the assessments section, but having a clear understanding of your current state of affairs matched up to where you want to be in a future state will be important. The one way to get there is to perform an assessment of existing tools in the environment and how they mesh with a framework of security controls like NIST CSF and then identify where your gaps exist from a tools, process, and people standpoint. This will allow the organization to fill those identified gaps and then move in the right direction for a future state.

Chapter 15

The Middle East

This case was very interesting. I was hired by a company to help conduct incident response that led into a larger investigation to determine the root cause and origin of the incident. There was a time when it wasn't uncommon for third-party applications and programs to send reporting information to other third parties. In some cases, the actual contracts would include language suggesting that information reporting could occur to third parties, including the company that owns the software or hardware. In some cases, companies did not identify these statements, and therefore, their information to a certain degree would end up in someone else's hands and, in some cases, unknown exactly the type of information the third party was actually receiving.

This case started out based on reports of fraudulent activity to employees' bank accounts and credit card accounts and, in some cases, all-out identity theft on tax returns and other activity. At first, the company dismissed it and claimed the activity was coincidental and likely do to their own mistakes or phishing against personal e-mail accounts or a half dozen other ways that bad people glean personal information from other people (victims). As time passed and more employees were reporting fraud, the legal department of the company became suspicious and called in the company's CSO to discuss and determine if, possibly, the fraud was a result of something done at the company. Now it was too coincidental that almost one hundred employees had reported fraudulent activity. The CSO set out to conduct an investigation by interviewing each of the employees that had reported the activity over the past several months. The CSO had told me when he hired me that the fraud activity wasn't targeting just one type of account, but the patterns were indicating different accounts for each person, and in a small number of cases, the individual's complete identity was stolen that went on to affect Social Security and IRS tax returns through fraudsters filing fake returns through tax software. The CSO performed a review of each IT project that had taken place over the previous six months to try and identify if a particular new software, hardware, SaaS, or other service could account for the fraud activity identified. The CSO called the PMO office as well to again look back over the last six to eight months for anything that could identify how all these employees were affected—nothing was found. The CSO brought in the internal audit team to conduct interviews of the affected employees to try and determine new information maybe missed by the CSO and his team. An additional approach to different questions were asked of the employees, but again, no new information was learned from the additional interviews.

I was hired to conduct a new investigation by an independent third party, and now everyone and everything at the company was fair game. The CSO sent communication to all business leaders, introducing me and my role for this project and that I was to have full access to all employees' information, and anything I requested access to would be granted without haste. I decided to take a different approach to the case. I would have agreed that by the CSO talking with PMO about all projects that maybe likely they would have identified the culprit. Having been employed at companies over the last thirty years, we always seem to run into the rogue individuals, shadow IT, and the departments that just decide on their own to do what they want because they don't like structure and they hate Big Brother to a point that they do what they want. Oh, and if there are consequences to their actions, they come up with an excuse that they think will get them out of the mess.

In review of the employees affected by some sort of activity, I noticed some patterns that made me think a bit. First off, the last names of the employees appeared to range between the letter M and P and verified that the information affected involved financial accounts and/or information that could be utilized by a bad actor to gain access to those accounts or steal from those accounts. Based on this information, I contacted the CFO for an interview as it would seem to me that the information, all PII, and tied to financial activity was likely the result of someone within his team. I also reached out to the CHRO to do the same as the information obtained by the bad actors could have originated with a payroll system, and not knowing whether HR or finance owned that function, I decided to interview both of them. I did determine that HR managed the payroll system but that finance was the budget owner for the solution. In talking with both leaders, they were unaware of any solution that could have caused the issue; they both reiterated that they had no projects in the last nine months that involved employee data. I informed them that I would be reaching out to their direct reports to conduct further interviews and fact-finding discussions. Both leaders fully supported my efforts and told me that I could reach out in case any of their employees were not cooperative.

I began walking around the finance area to get a determination of the people working in the department, conversations, and the lay of the land. I would talk to people on the spot, without notice, walk around desks and working areas to see what was what, walk past offices gleaning conversations among coworkers and guests that might have been visiting. The finance department seemed to have a wide age range of employees: some long term, been with the company for more than fifteen years; many interns trying to gain experience; and other mid-level, middle-aged employees doing just about the "middle of the road" from a performance perspective. These were the individuals that I was interested in meeting and talking to and see where it would lead me. In one of the conversations I had with a manager of the department, she was somewhat concerned regarding another employee, happened to be one of those employees that I was interested to talk to. I asked this manager why she was so concerned with this other employee that she actually did not even manage directly, let alone indirectly. The manager mentioned that the employee had only been with the company for six months and had already taken three PTO periods, averaging in length of about a week a piece. In one of the instances, the manager mentioned that a mutual coworker had commented that the "target individual" had traveled extensively outside the United States, to foreign countries mostly in the Middle East. Now I was starting to get engaged and really interested in talking with this individual. The manager also commented that she thought the target might be in the wrong department as other employees had commented previously that the target employee is always talking about technology, automation, machine-learning capabilities, and the fact that he wants to make his mark in the industry as a techie guru. Hmm, now I was very intrigued.

I reported my initial findings to the CSO and requested that he work with HR to pull the target's HR file, including background report and any additional information. I also informed the CSO that I was going to have some discussions with law enforcement contacts to try and ascertain any information about the target, especially if he was on any agency's radar at present. I found that the target, while employed with the company, had visited the Middle East four times in the past six months, none for company business but personal vacations. All travel was while using his own passport for the trips. He always listed the same address while in country within the Middle East. Many third-party applications that I had tested or tried out in the past were all originating in certain Middle East countries. These countries have produced some brilliant techie minds and some fantastic applications and technology still in use throughout companies and governments all around the world. The one thing I did remember from my assessing and testing of the solutions, these companies always placed a back door of reporting that would lead to the home office in country to keep tabs on the company, learn about company traffic, business being conducted, statistics, and metrics, which was always the reason these companies gave as to why the third-party reporting was installed in the first place. I reached out to some in-country contacts that might have the opportunity or availability of providing more information about the target. I had also learned that the target was planning to visit some of these countries in the coming months, and that might lend an opportunity for in-country surveillance by my contacts.

I requested the CSO to run some reports and inquiries related to web traffic and firewall traffic and any additional tools/tech he had at his disposal that could identify any suspicious activity on the network tied to the employee (target) credentials. I sat down with the target for an interview to gather more information about the employee. My real intent was to try and understand what the target did for the company, what his motivations might be, what he wants to do in the future, etc. My initial thoughts on the target were that he seemed disgruntled, unaware of why that was. After chatting a bit in a very laid-back manner, the target started to discuss how his primary interest at the company was working in the IT department as he was very fond of technology and the change in the industry and how certain applications might be helpful to a company like this one. The target also talked about his love of Middle East and that he had a friend that owned a tech company there that provides financial-type applications for businesses, but he had yet to gain traction in the United States. The target continued to tell me that he was trying to assist his friend with his goals by introducing his friend with other companies in the United States and that he did the same at this company, but the powers that be claimed they were not in need of this type of application. I completed this initial interview with a direction in mind, and I thanked the target for making the time.

I went back and spoke to the CSO about the initial findings and a proposed direction. We needed to ascertain through the existing payroll or other systems that held employee PII whether any connections or APIs were installed or developed between the system and an unknown application. The CSO reached out to the application owners to determine that. I reviewed some of the firewall and network reports related to the user in question, and there were some evidence of activity with his credentials related to a third-party application that provides (after research) financial and payroll reporting services for a client. The application was built and owned by a company in the Middle East, and there were some threat intelligence reports detailing indications that the application owner was using his application to breach networks and companies without their knowledge and then exfiltrating or, in many cases, transmitting the data back to Middle Eastern countries through a cloud provider. Network anomaly tools and firewall reports were able to identify when the application was installed on the network and the location which was consistent with the target's computer and credentials. The CSO also learned that API connectors were set up by a contractor (that was no longer employed by the company) to share the personnel data with the application, and the target used what he thought was a sample snapshot of data (from a file created by the ex-contractor) that actually was live employee PII. Activity indicated that once the target likely figured out that the data was actual live personnel data, the APIs were disconnected, and the application stopped.

I rescheduled another meeting with the employee to discuss the findings and ascertain any additional information. I also requested that the CSO to seize the target's computer so that a forensic examination could be conducted to show the application usage and likely removal of the application from the employee computer system.

The interview with the target confirmed that he acted in a way that he thought he could prove to his manager and leaders that the application his friend told him about could really save the company money in the long run and would be beneficial to the business. The target admitted that he really did not know what he was doing with regard to the application and he was unaware that the application created a back door/gateway into the corporate network and that the application was sending company data to his friend's company.

CHAPTER 15

Case in Review and Recommendations

After the interview with the target in this case, I would refer to this type of insider threat as "negligent insider"; these were typically employees or contractors working for the company that even though their actions may have caused a breach or a security incident where information was disclosed or exposed to others that were not authorized to see or view the data, the individuals (insider threat) did not act in a malicious manner but rather with negligence. I found in my history of conducting investigations that you find insiders that are either too lazy or maybe they are overworked. They code an application incorrectly, they don't check their work, and then the application malfunctions by e-mailing customer data to an unknown third party. It happens, but as a company, decisions must be determined on how to react to a security incident to ensure you are meeting your contractual obligations and, also important, any legal, compliance, and/or regulatory requirements.

Recommendations:

1. Network Visibility - There are specific tools that can assist with increasing your visibility of network traffic in your environment. Much like a user behavior analytics tool, there are similar for examining network traffic flows so that further determinations and verifications can be made on what traffic is authorized and what traffic may be suspicious. Network visibility monitoring and tools can help identify exfiltration points (cyber kill chain and MITRE Att&ck framework tactics) where data may be lost through unauthorized methods. These factors could also help indicate areas of improvement or additional security controls, such as implementing stronger controls, monitoring, and systems, such as data loss prevention (DLP) technology.

2. Employee Behavior - Managers have the responsibility to uphold company policy and standards and ensure that their direct reports are adhering to company policies and guidelines. If the manager spotted possible behavior issues with the employee, he/she should have escalated the concern to HRBP and/or contact security to discuss the concerns. It's far greater and better to raise concerns, no matter if the concern seems stupid or a non-issue; let the professionals determine if the concern was real before it manifests into a larger and serious issue for the company. Security leaders should push to keep relationships with business stakeholders open and clear with communication and a two-way channel to ensure ongoing support and collaboration.

3. Data Loss Prevention - If the company had implemented a data security strategy, including the use of data loss prevention (DLP), then the employee PII data would likely not have been transmitted outside the corporate network and quarantined as part of the process for a DLP system in operation.

4. Data Security Strategy - It is important for any organization operating in an area with sensitive information (customer data and/or employee data, among other types) to have a well-established data security strategy—the people behind the program, the tools that should be deployed within the network to enforce the strategy and prevent data leakage along with proper processes and policy, including the coveted data classification policy and the standards required for protecting sensitive data—at rest, in use and in transit.

Chapter 16

Third-Party Risk Is Real

This next case and investigation involved a financial service company that I had performed some consulting for in the past. The financial service firm utilized a third-party shared service offshore provider in the West Indies and Asia Pacific for performing outbound and inbound sales calls to customers. The credit card operations division of the company signed contracts with various offshore companies to augment the staff as the business did not have the ability to hire the number of staff needed.

My client (corporate security department) was never notified by this business unit of the third parties at hand. There was corporate policy that dictated third-party risk program and assessment for all third-party companies at all times. My client was eventually notified by the credit card operations group leader that a disgruntled employee at one of these offshore companies had gone back to their office, damaged, vandalized, and forced open their data center, and stole a server that belonged to my client's company. This server had customer information and some of that sensitive data. Not only was an incident determined because of the stolen information on the server and the theft violated several data breach privacy laws for a variety of US states where those customers resided, but also, it was determined that other protections might not have been implemented on the server to protect the data itself. The initial investigation and inquiry with the business unit determined that the business unit went ahead with hiring several offshore third parties that would be working with customer PII and PCI data but did not adhere to company policy to ensure that a third-party assessment was conducted. Contracts were signed with these companies, and business started without knowing what risks might be present. The business unit leader commented that she did not think it was necessary to have a risk assessment since the companies she was using were also used by many big brand companies, and she figured that if those companies hired these offshore companies, then they must be okay.

As part of my inquiry, I reviewed all contracts and agreements between the company and the three vendors that were used by this business unit. In initial phone discussions to ascertain what their security posture looked like or what security controls they had in place, not surprisingly, it was found that there was an extreme lack of security measures and controls in place. I explained to each vendor that in order to continue conducting business, they would be required to undergo onsite audits and review of all aspects of security and agree to remediate any gaps or issues identified. Two of the vendors were reluctant, and the business leader was also upset that all transactions had to stop until these audits were completed and issues remediated. After several meetings with the business leader, one an in-person meeting with her, she was better equipped and understood the importance of a third-party risk assessment and ensuring these and other third parties dealing with/handling PII and PCI data be properly assessed and approved before we conduct business. As it was, the vendor whom the server was stolen from had serious issues with security:

1. Lack of or no physical security controls of data center area where servers were located.
2. Lack of or no CCTV coverage for egress/ingress as well as sensitive locations like data center locations and other areas where sensitive data was stored.
3. No data security measures in use, including no data at rest or data in transit encryption protocols in use.

4. No background checks conducted on employees handling sensitive data.
5. Lack of company policy and standards surrounding physical and information security.

The only information known by the vendor was the identity of the employee that broke into the server room and stole the server belonging to the company. I contacted local in-country law enforcement to ensure that a report was filed at the least. The vendor claimed they made calls to the employee to understand why the server was taken, but the employee failed to return calls.

Over the following two months, I made a series of overseas trips to visit with the various vendors hired by the business leader to conduct onsite audits and security assessments, meet with the vendor contacts and security representatives, and interview employees related to the assessments. I put together each assessment report per vendor and location with a list of the gaps requiring immediate remediation that would be sufficient for the business to continue transacting with the company. This also included onsite visits to all offshore facilities, a visit when the initial assessment was conducted, and a follow-up visit after remediation was concluded by each facility and vendor.

CHAPTER 16
Case in Review and Recommendations

Third-party risk is an issue that many companies still face, even with the numerous cyber breaches that have spread across the news and the Internet ever since some of the initial breaches discovered in 2013. Third-party risk became the major highlight for companies across the globe to ensure their third parties were meeting certain obligations to ensure that their customer's sensitive data was protected at all times. Many companies in every industry started to adopt a series of processes and policies to ensure that new business with a third party was met with a consistent assessment process and a decision as to whether that vendor could continue business with a company. Industry standards had been developed that could be utilized by an entity in the assessment of a third party—security questionnaires, a list of documents that a company might own that could be reviewed (e.g., prior risk assessments, SOC 2 reports, etc.), and even using third-party SaaS providers that could assess the top level posture of a company using scanning software.

Recommendations:

1. Ensure your organization utilizes an established and documented third-party risk assessment process and policy. Educate all business stakeholders and leaders into the process and when to engage the assessment. Coordinate and educate the same with your procurement department as they will sometimes become aware of a third-party relationship before you do.
2. Include mentions of third-party risk assessments into other company documents, including information security policy and standards, and it could act as a stand-alone standard for third-party risk assessments.
3. Coordinate with company PMOs and architect services as many times these two groups may become aware of projects and new

vendors before security or GRC teams are made aware. Educate these teams regarding the need for third-party risk assessments.

4. Configuration standards are important for any hardware assets that will especially include any sensitive data being stored on the asset. Remember any sensitive data should be protected per a data security strategy that includes controls and measures for ensuring that all data in transit, in use, and at rest are always protected no matter what.

5. Third Party - Minimum Data Security Requirements - This is additional language that would be added to your contracts, MSAs, and other agreements. This is language in the form of your organization's requirements for data security that the vendor or third party must adhere to in order to conduct business with the organization.

6. The right to audit should be included in your contracts and agreements with third-party vendors and the right to annual risk assessments and onsite/offsite audits of the requirements surrounding data security, including visiting the company when needed to conduct your own check and balances to ensure continued compliance.

Chapter 17

Someone Was Listening

The fear that your competitor or another government is listening in on conversations and gathering important information is a risk of any company, especially if your company sells a special technology not developed by others or even the same analogy with a technology developed by a company that a particular government wants to have access to. If you talk to government intelligence analysts and operational specialists, you might find it intriguing that this form of spying by a country against a country is so commonplace today across the globe. In some cases, even each participant knows clearly well if it is happening without any hesitation. In some environments that are highly regulated, there are certain security measures that can be utilized - specialized and secure rooms, also called a SCIF - Sensitive Compartmented Information Facility used by the government and the many federal contractor companies employed by the governments, or through highly specialized investigations and preventative measures used to identify unauthorized spying through a concept known as TSCM -Technical Security Countermeasures - use of various tools and technologies to sweep rooms and areas looking for bugs (used for spying on others).

In this particular case, the client company held board meetings in a particular location each and every time within the corporate headquarters and the only place designated for these meetings. As a regular cadence, the investigations group conducted TSCM sweeps of executive vehicles, offices, and board room spaces to ensure they were clear of wiretapping devices—both of audio and video origin. Nowadays, there are so many ways to hide these devices that could be difficult to identify in some cases.

On a particular day, while a sweep was being conducted in the boardroom, a new vendor appeared in the boardroom lobby requesting access prior to the meeting to set up audio-visual equipment that was ordered for the meeting. The boardroom lobby has a receptionist area, but instead of a receptionist, the company had specific security staff manning this area at all times to ensure only authorized individuals were granted access. The staff member on duty at the time of the incident was unaware of a "new" company providing A/V equipment because all previous times, a different company offered the services. The security staff member requested documentation and proof of purchase by a company representative to get to the bottom of why a new company was in use and why no one communicated this to security. The A/V company apparently checked out and was allowed access to the area but with an escort, which I don't think the guys that were present were wanting an escort. Security staff contacted a supervisor for that very fact because the lead A/V person had requested that they be allowed to work with an escort—suspicious.

It was decided that we would conduct surveillance on this A/V company while they were setting up for the board meeting within the meeting room area. Security and investigations had areas within the facility to carry our covert surveillance as needed, which was usually during the actual event or meeting, not pre-planning or set up. The team got into position, while the vendor entered the room and started their preparations to set up the technology equipment, screens, projectors, microphones, etc. As the vendor was setting up their equipment, one of the surveillance analysts noted that two of the vendor representatives were acting suspicious with regard to certain areas of the room they were accessing, that were not really part of their scope for the set up of equipment. I went into the room to have a discussion with the two individuals that were acting suspicious, questioning what it was that they were doing in the two areas the surveillance team noted they accessed without permission or business need. Upon questioning, the individuals stated they were unaware there were areas they were not allowed to access and plainly commented that they entered by mistake when they say there was nothing in the rooms related to the set up of their equipment. I asked the TSCM team to sweep both rooms immediately while the vendor was present. I also requested my client to contact the vendor and speak to a manager about the individuals that were on site installing the equipment as I was surprised there was no supervisor from the vendor company present. The TSCM team immediately relayed that they had positive hits for wiretapping devices installed in the two rooms that our surveillance team witnessed.

My client was calling me at the same time about an urgent issue. Upon reaching my client, she had a director of customer care from the vendor on the phone. My client indicated that the vendor company was unaware of the company (client) as well confirmed he did not send any teams to install A/V equipment at our location. At this point, I contacted my local law enforcement contacts and requested they respond as we had individuals not only claiming to be employees of this vendor but they were also installing wiretapping devices. My contacts asked some questions and responded they would be out ASAP. I had the client alert all his security and investigation teams of the issue and to also speak with his executive protection leader that they should move the board meeting to a different location as there had been a breach and it was being handled and investigated. They agreed and would help the executive teams plan another location out of harm's way.

I returned to the board room area where the vendor was still in process of "setting up" equipment. I checked in with the surveillance teams, and they reported what appeared to be normal activity by the vendors. I asked the vendors about how long they would be on site, and they responded by saying they needed another hour. I commented that would be good and let me know if they have any requests or needs. I reached out to the physical security monitoring group and requested CCTV footage showing/detailing the vendor arriving at the premises, etc., as well requested to have a guard go out in the parking lot and record identifying information about the vehicle, including license plate, VIN, etc.

I returned to the board room area where the vendor targets were still setting up. By this time, law enforcement had arrived on scene, and I went to meet them at the lower lobby level. I provided background information and how I was able to ascertain that the individuals upstairs were bad actors but also recent TSCM sweeps conducted while the targets were in the building. I escorted law enforcement agents to the board room area, and they began their inquiry into the individuals that we identified from the fake vendor.

It was later determined that the individuals had not only attempted to set up throwaway wiretapping devices, meaning they were designed to be identified or spotted and would be removed accordingly, but they had also set up (or attempted to set up) stationary devices into areas that could pick up audio and video in some cases but would be more difficult to identify through scanning processes. The devices apparently mimicked normal Ghz readings and other factors and could appear to be normal communication devices. The individuals were interviewed by law enforcement on scene, and one of the individuals did, in fact, provide context surrounding their visit (a.k.a. cooperated with officials). It was determined that the individuals were hired by a competitor to install listening devices for the purposes of theft of information and to gain ways of improving their business decisions based on the decisions discussed by the company (victim).

CHAPTER 17

Case Review and Recommendations

As a security professional and depending on your area of expertise and/or area of responsibility, protecting your company, government, or other entity is a typical responsibility that cannot be taken lightly. Depending on the scenarios of private meetings and such where discussions of sensitive information, if things get in the wrong hands, it could prove to be detrimental to your organization. Proper measures and controls are necessary to prevent and deter such incidents from happening. This case was no different as the company was a constant target by many special interest groups and disgruntled individuals, treating all threats, whether real or possible, as serious until further determination can be made on whether the threat was actionable or informational.

Recommendations:

1. Depending on your organization, especially if you are a public company, implementing a formal TSCM program and conducting regular sweeps of your executive's offices, board rooms, and residential locations, ensure that no unauthorized listening/wiretapping devices are present. If you don't have staff with the expertise, always hire a third party with this specialized experience.

2. Threat Intelligence Program - There are a variety of types of threat intelligence programs that may come into play in your organization. The two at the top of the list are cyber threat intelligence and physical threat intelligence, usually of the activist, extremist, anarchist kind, and/or special interest groups and individuals that might be targeting your organization. Having an individual and/or team in place to address these threats (cyber, letters, mail, packages, in person, groups,

protests) will be vital to your organization and keeping your assets (employees and executives) safe and secure and aware of danger.

3. Increased security at public meetings, including board meetings or annual board meetings, is important. Having in-person/ on-site security personnel (both dressed and in plain clothes), following protocols for executive protection, live threat intelligence screening and monitoring, and other controls and measures in place will certainly assist your organization in a decreased chance of issues and incidents.

4. Partnering with your investor committee will be important when it comes to planning of the board meeting/annual board meeting. In some cases and from experience, if the executives and/or board members were experiencing threats, we would move the meeting location to a hotel or other facility. In many cases, we would work with the organizers to review a list of attendees prior to the event so that we could identify any potential problems we might face at the event.

5. For any third-party vendors involved in sensitive events, such as a board meeting, always ensure that when a vendor shows up at your facility, they are who they say they are. Establishing authentication measures and/or controls between your organization and your vendor might be necessary as well to ensure authorized personnel are working in your facilities, especially during sensitive matters.

6. Ensure your organization has visitor controls in place, including escort requirements, depending on the visitor to your organization. Also, if an escort is required, ensure that an escort is assigned at all times, no matter what. If you let someone walk your facility without an escort, even once, could present an issue from a security standpoint. It is also a good opportunity to communicate when vendors are present in the facility and to remind employees to ensure they protect sensitive data while visitors are in the facility.

Chapter 18

A Mining We Will Go

Just when you thought you have seen everything then this type of case rears its ugly head. Initial thoughts about this case were simply an employee abuse of Internet/violation of company acceptable use policy, but as time went on and more effort to investigate, additional information led us to a much larger issue and one that many companies might face from time to time.

On occasion, my client would get a call from an HRBP (human resources business partner) regarding network bandwidth issues caused by employee or user overuse of the Internet/network resources, and there would be a request to investigate the type of usage by the user and all pertinent information. My client CSO called me and asked if I was available to handle an investigation into this new matter.

The company did have an acceptable use policy (AUP) that all employees and contractors had to sign and agree with on an annual basis. Network bandwidth issues were an ongoing issue, especially at office locations where the Internet bandwidth may have been less, and some employees affected could certainly feel the difference when someone was hogging the bandwidth.

In this case, HRBP and the client CSO met with me to provide information about several complaints regarding bandwidth usage issues in one of the field offices, and several employees could not utilize certain applications because of this issue. I immediately started to investigate the issue, starting with firewall traffic analysis for the field office in question, based on the user data that was provided through human resources. As a general rule, there was certain activity that the company did not permit (network usage and certain protocols) and also alerted on through their SIEM when anomalies were present and/or suspicious behaviors. Based on traffic analysis of the user in question, it was determined that only during certain time frames was the user engaged in high network bandwidth usage, and it had been going on for several months. The traffic would start around 3:00 PM local time to the field office and extend through the night and into the morning and cease around 7:00 AM local time.

I was interested to see what the user's job code and description was to try and first understand if there was a logical reason for this type of network bandwidth requirement, e.g., regular reporting to a third-party website or other regular work or traffic requiring the bandwidth. The user's position was of a financial analyst, and there would really be no need for this sort of traffic requirement. I checked in with local IT personnel in the field to identify any requests that may have been made recently by the user, of which there were none, except the user had put in request for an electrical strip as his office only had one outlet. I didn't really think much of that request, so it went to the back of my head. I went back to the traffic, web usage, and firewall reports to review and try and determine anything useful. After an initial review of the reports, it would appear that the user was directing traffic on multiple devices to multiple destinations for the entire time frame identified. After a review of the destination locations, I was able to determine that the sites in question were all Bitcoin-mining sites.

I immediately booked travel to go visit the employee target in question. I also reached out to facilities and requested their electricity bills for the last six months and whether there were any spikes in usage over the six-month period, and if so, did they report it to anyone. I scheduled an interview with the employee, calling it an informational session as I was trying to identify various local managers and their roles, almost like a census exercise. The target agreed to the meeting at his office.

I arrived in the field location and drove to the office. I met the target in his office, and the first thing that was interesting to me was the number of computers he had set up in his office. His work laptop was set up on his desk, but he had three other tower desktops set up around his room. While I sat in the office waiting for the target to get back from the bathroom, I snapped photos of the devices and sent an e-mail to local IT contact to ascertain how many computing devices had been assigned to the target over the course of his employment. The target returned, and we started the meeting. It was more of a meet and greet to understand what he was responsible for in the scheme of things. The target explained he was a finance analyst for a particular business unit within the company and was recently assigned to this field office location. He had relocated his family, of which the company did reimburse for, but the target told me in confidence that he was struggling a bit. I mentioned to the target that I consult for the client company on third-party risk, and if there were vendors you were doing business with, that the client company had a formal program and process to assess them. The target commented that his other previous clients had similar processes, so he was very familiar with them. I said great and was getting ready to leave the room when I had to ask about the extra computers. The target told me an elaborate story about some of the financial processes and tasks that were operationalized recently and the additional computing power necessary to accomplish the reporting to the SEC as required by the government for public companies. I responded by saying that it sounds very complicated and glad he had a good handle on the requirements. I thanked him for his time and left the field office. By that time, IT had gotten back and also told me that the target had ordered additional computers that were going to be used for specialized financial operations and transaction processing and required by compliance regulations. I asked IT to send me the original request form with the target's signature on it, authorizing the expenditure and the reason for it.

I had a phone call with my client to discuss an update on the case, and I made a request to "trap and trace" on the field office Internet connection, as I wanted to gain further insight into the specific activity performed by the target, although I already had a pretty good idea of what was happening. Normally, if law enforcement wanted to conduct a trap and trace on a line, they were required to have a court order, National Security letter, or subpoena. Even though this client was a corporate entity, they still adhered to best practices and included some level of checks and balances (best practices) when we were going to conduct eavesdropping on Internet connections. I had utilized a specialized team that would conduct the eavesdropping, and they were dispatched out to the field office area to conduct the work needed. I provided the local IT contact as well since they would be needed to show the team to the telco closet. The team went forward with trapping the line to determine additional evidence of suspicious activity by the target.

I returned to the hotel and, by that time, had received reports from the facilities department and an urgent call from the head of facilities, asking me to reach back out. I contacted the head of facilities, and he explained that maybe he should have done a better job in monitoring bills and usage because and only because of my request was he able to now see there was a huge spike in electricity for the field office for the last four to five months since the complaints began, etc. I told him that I would review the electricity bills and reports that he sent over. I asked him not to do anything as of right now but that there would be a conclusion soon and electricity usage would return to normal. The reports and information indicated normal electrical usage about six months prior when all activity was normal. I was then able to review and determine the difference between normal activity and the surges in service so that I could apply a monetary amount for losses associated with the case. The losses were in the tens of thousands of dollars, so it was a huge impact from a budgetary and monetary standpoint, along with the abuse of services and inappropriate use of corporate assets and networks. Even without the trap-and-trace activity, I was able to determine, after review of network traffic/firewall traffic, network flow information and now the associated electricity usage that the target was involved with Bitcoin-mining operation that he was running from his office. I was also able to determine that the traffic originating from the desktop machines were, in fact, not conducting any legitimate network traffic as indicated by the target during the initial interview.

The next day I set up an interview with the target but this time chose a conference room within the HR department at the field office. The target did, in fact, accept the meeting request, and he showed up on time. This time I was overt about the meeting context and introduced myself with my actual role and how I worked with the client CSO. I could see from the behavior exhibited by the target, between the time he entered the room and when I told him my real job, he sort of knew why I was there. I continued with the interview and advised the target of company ethics policy and participation in corporate investigations in a truthful manner, and he signed the policy affirmation document before the crux of the interview continued. I asked the target again about the extra computers in his office and asked if he wanted to change his story from our initial meeting; at which time the target did, in fact, say to the affirmative that he wasn't very honest the first time. By the end of the interview, the target provided a written accounting (confession) of the activity he was performing from his office over the prior four months. The employee asked what would happen to him as far as employment was concerned. I explained that HR will be in touch with him. I told him that because he was honest (to a point) that that fact would be counted toward efforts to participate in the investigation honestly, etc. I did explain that the company would not be pursuing any criminal action against him since, in reality, there was no crime besides theft of services which he would have to agree to reimburse the company as long as he stayed employed for at least the next year, and if not, then the company could file civil charges against him for repayment of losses.

Case Review and Recommendations

I remember when this particular case came about, and after I understood the context better as far as what I was dealing with in relation to the target, around this time, there was an increase in these types of cases across the industry. I remember having these discussions with other peers and clients and the talk of approach to dealing with this issue of not only the misuse of corporate assets and network but also the suggestive liability issues if activity was tracked back to the company and/or any cyberattacks against the company because the traffic was tracked back to the employee and/or the company as a whole. Most companies need the Internet to conduct business and, as such, provide this privilege to employees to use sparingly and according to internal policy and standards, including an acceptable use policy (AUP), which is very similar to the same AUP or terms of service that a user of Internet services would sign when they begin their service with the Internet service provider (ISP). The fact is when the corporate environment has access to the Internet and it's left open for all sorts of activity, then abuse will occur and sparks a good conversation about blocking and controlling access on the Internet to certain websites, services, applications, and protocols. This particular case was a good lesson to learn and identify areas that we could improve upon, especially with proactively blocking firewall traffic/network traffic as it pertained to activity that should not be allowed on work computers/company network.

Recommendations:

1. Security monitoring through SIEM (security incident and event manager) is important to understand and have visibility with concern to what activity is occurring over your network and within your network infrastructure. Responding to alerts in

a timely manner and remediating these issues is important too. While this particular case was not necessarily involving an alertable offense, there could have been alerts related to cyberattacks, attack tactics, trends, and other threats that could have been due to the target's activity over the network and beyond into cyberspace. Mining for Bitcoin is a very competitive "sport," and there have been numerous articles about Bitcoin heists and thefts over the years.

2. Make a decision early to block certain protocols, ports, traffic, applications, and websites that would never be appropriate for the workplace and/or could present undue security risk and privacy concerns for the company and/or legal issues. In the future, if there are reasons for a user or a business that needs access to a restricted service, an exception would be documented, if approved. As an example, Bitcoin-mining activity uses TCP and ports 8080 and 8081 and sometimes 8333. There will be a need to investigate additional tactics in use to ensure that those protocols are blocked.

3. Additional IT Resource Requests - IT departments should ensure that proper assessment and process is in place to ensure that additional computer requests by any employee is a recognized requirement for their position and job and that appropriate leadership sign off on these requests. In addition, this investigation found that IT did not implement a review of the claimed third-party usage originally documented by the target on his request form. Follow up with IT leadership (with trickle down awareness) was made to ensure this scenario did not happen again.

4. Threat Hunting - More and more organizations are employing threat hunters as part of security operations center (SOC) business and/or within cyber threat intelligence duties within the security department. Threat hunters typically work off already-received alerts from SIEM, trends from SIEM, prior incidents and security events, and sometimes just random hunting in places where there might be suspicious activity.

5. User Behavior Analytics - This is an additional tool that could be helpful in these types of situations as they provide a baseline risk profile based on previous activity, and then as risky situations become known, their risk profile changes, which could allow alerting of suspicious activity that requires further investigation to deem whether it is normal or abnormal activity.

Chapter 19

The Old Fake Vendor Scam

At this one client, I worked mostly external crime cases. On occasion, I was asked to work complex internal cases as well. I welcomed a good challenge with any investigation as sometimes it was necessary to think outside the box, outwit the targets attempting to defraud the company or think they got away with their master crime.

The client CSO was proud about his relationship with business stakeholders and how they would proactively reach to him when needed. This particular business unit was an accounting division, handling accounts receivables and accounts payables for a multitude of business divisions within the company. The accounting corps, as they liked to call themselves, consisted of multiple four-person groups that would handle either receivables processing or payables operations. The manager mentioned that she was experiencing some troubles with one of her staff members, always seemed to be against everyone else and thought that Big Brother was after everyone and that the company acted like Big Brother too, etc. The manager also mentioned that a coworker had reported to her that the target was telling other coworkers that he found a way that he could steal money from the company without anyone knowing it, and by the time they did realize it, he would be long gone outside the country, in a country that had no treaty with the United States and blah, blah, blah. The manager mentioned that the target was, in fact, leaving for vacation (unsure where) in less than two weeks, so time was of the essence.

The client asked me to investigate this case and that I would have access to any records or personnel that I would require. I pulled the target's HR file to identify if there were any foreign countries that he might go to or visit because of family. Sometimes this information could be found in the HR file or other employee files and notes, especially e-mails if the employee had submitted vacation request and listed the location they would be traveling to. I also conducted a full background investigation on the target, including key log audit (some positions/ employees would have keyloggers attached to workstations for security and auditing reasons) and web usage to identify anything out of the ordinary and/or behavior. I then scheduled some confidential interviews with the target's coworkers to learn more about the target, his working behavior, and anything personal. As I would meet with his coworkers, they were advised that they could not speak about the investigation to anyone, and if they did, in fact, they could face disciplinary action up to and including termination. Each employee agreed, and interviews proceeded with majority of the coworkers knowing the target was heading on vacation—back to his homeland in Asia. The target's parents apparently lived in both the United States and Asia, but his parents were apparently not traveling to Asia this time. One of the coworkers corroborated the story, the same story that the manager had heard about, where the target claimed that he found a way to steal money without anyone knowing it. Most of the coworkers had stated that the target was very cocky and "full of himself" and felt like he was entitled all the time.

I went back to review the background reports, key log audit reports, and other data I had pulled. Some of his Internet search history confirmed that he may be traveling to Asian countries as there was heavy search history for events and things to do in particular beach towns during the same time he was planning to go. There was also a search history where the target had accessed his flight confirmation and flight details for the trip to Asia, so I now had some confirmation on flight information. I also decided to pull a forensic copy of his hard drive over the network so that I had additional evidence should I require.

In the key log audit, there appeared to be some anomalous behavior with some of his transactions, including some of the financial payouts to "invoices" that did not make sense. I contacted the manager (of the target) and asked her to research some of the companies connected to the strange behavior and to let me know what type of customer they were and what sort of services we provided and vice versa, where they providing us services and, if so, to whom in the company and what were the services they were paying for. I also asked the manager to reach out to the companies rather than through e-mails to ask the questions. Roughly ten minutes after hanging up the phone, the manager called me back to inform me that none of the phone numbers worked, and she was unable to contact any human being at those companies identified. I then requested the manager to track all payments that were paid to the three suspicious companies, dates, and exact amounts of the payments that were processed by the target. The manager told me it would take a few hours and that she would forward the information to me as soon as she had the list. I had a feeling here and wanted some context before I went digging.

At this point, I wanted to have an information-gathering interview (less formal) with the employee, get to know them and their job and that sort of thing. I scheduled some time with the employee over the phone, and he agreed, and we were able to get together rather quickly. I scheduled a conference room near his working space so he wouldn't have to go that far. I met with the target, and as expected, he was coming across as if entitled and bothered by the meeting, claiming he had too much work to do and I was wasting his time—not a good start to the meeting. The target wanted to know why an investigator like myself was meeting with him and then claimed he had done nothing wrong. I hadn't even started asking any questions, and already, the target was defensive. I simply told the target that I was talking to several employees in the area to find out if anyone had heard anything nefarious going on among coworkers. The target quickly answered no and asked if he could leave the room. I was intrigued and wanted to know more and asked the target why he was in such a hurry. The target responded and commented, "I don't give a crap, and I am not a snitch," and then he got up and walked out. I thanked him for his time as he was leaving the room. To me, his reactions were a great start to this case, and I was definitely keeping him as the primary target of the case. As soon as I returned to my desk, the manager had the printout of the transactions for payables that were processed by the target connected to the three suspicious companies. The total aggregate amount of money that was paid out was roughly $300,000 over a three-month period. I contacted the audit group and requested an internal auditor to review the target's bank account transactions (deposits, withdrawals, transfers, other accounts, etc.,) and to put together a summary and send it to me. I had a few other things to do, and I wanted to have some help from the audit group (as they were always trying to be helpful, so I figured, why not?) to gather the info. I also asked for a snapshot of the target's accounts over the last four months. The audit review of his bank accounts and transactions confirmed my suspicions that the target had, in fact, siphoned money by misappropriation through the fake vendor invoices and stupidly deposited the funds into his personal bank accounts in the same and exact dollar amounts indicated on the ledger reports provided by the manager. The money in aggregate of $300,000 was still present in the bank accounts.

I conducted a second interview with the target based on the information identified so far in the investigation. The target flat-out denied the scam and could not explain the money in his bank accounts, except that his parents had given him the money for some reason. I told the target that I would be verifying his statements and claims of where the money came from. The employee then stated that he had nothing else to say and that I was off base on this one. I told the target I appreciated his time. The target then responded that, "I am heading out on vacation and would be gone for a couple of weeks. You have no evidence tying me to this alleged activity. Good luck."

I went back to my desk to make some calls as I needed to figure out where the employee was heading on his vacation. I also noted that the funds in the bank account had been removed the following day through a request at a local branch. I checked with HR to see if they held any identifiable documents on the target, of which we had a passport number and, of course, Social Security, date of birth, and driver's license information. I reached out to my local law enforcement contact regarding the case, but he was tied up with another case but acknowledged that I had sufficient information for warrants, and once he was done, he would submit paperwork to the court. He also told me to carry on with the investigation and he would catch up later. (This was the type of working relationship I had). I reached out to another contact at a law enforcement agency that had oversight over flights and was able to determine the itinerary for the target, which apparently was noted as highly suspicious as if the target was trying to elude authorities based on his numerous flight segments. His final destination was in South Asia, and the best choke point for me was his layover in Japan. I reached out to law enforcement contacts in Japan, advised them of the issue that the target would be traveling through their jurisdiction and that federal law enforcement was aware and if they could assist. My contact agreed and asked if I had any requests. I told my contact that I would be jumping on the next available plane to Japan, but if he could muster a team to meet the target at his gate, investigate why he was bringing excess money into the country. I surmised that the target would be hiding the $300,000 in his luggage based on a tip received from the target's coworker who overheard the target talking on the phone about his plan. Japanese authorities agreed that they would escort the target to a back office holding area and wait for me. I told them my main goal is to retrieve/seize the funds and let him go on his way at this time. The contact agreed with the strategy, and we would stay in touch.

By the time I arrived in Japan, the target had recently arrived and was snatched up by the authorities and had been taken to a holding area. The authorities questioned the target about a tip that he was carrying excessive cash on his person; at which time the target claimed he was not. His luggage was seized and inspected further, which did amount to the stolen funds packed into secret compartments within his luggage. The funds were removed, and his baggage was given back. I did visit him once before going on his way to let him know I was completely aware of his actions and that I was seizing the money. The target left on his next departure.

I flew back to the United States with the seized money. I was in contact with local law enforcement that informed me that arrest and search warrants were obtained. They also placed a hold notice on immigration so that once attempting to enter the United States on his return trip, he would be held and extradited back to the local area and arrested formally. I had the client CSO place a freeze on his bank accounts as well, with a note that any calls on the account could be referred to his office. Upon entry into New York a couple of weeks later, the target was held and arrested by officials.

Case in Review and Recommendations

This case background and context was very consistent with other similar cases discussed with industry peers and clients, and just based on articles about fake vendor profiles resulting in fraudulent payments and theft of money from a company, it's almost a trend that was constantly hitting the news for months at the time. This was the mid-2000s. As of now, these schemes have grown in size and complexity and, in some cases, still involve the initial foundation of this fake vendor scheme. The quick response to this issue was due to the old "see something, say something" attitude we have placed among citizens at the airport, the grocery, and at the workplace.

Recommendations:

1. "See Something, Say Something" - Besides talking about the responsibility of employees to report issues or concerns to their managers, HR, or other contacts, constant security awareness through posters, timed e-mail messages, and other formats are good ideas to keep this topic top of mind and to welcome self-reporting of issues anytime, even anonymously.

2. Vendor Management - Following this investigation and identifying a flaw in the vendor management system, an authentication process was put in place to ensure verification of new vendors was conducted once (after) the vendor was added to the ERP or other system. Have certain checks and balances to ensure compliance and legal requirements are met and also independent verification of the vendor contact details.

3. ERP Anomaly Monitoring and Reporting - In this case, three vendors were created in the system that all included the same payable bank account information and, on top of it, to a consumer-grade bank account as well. The verification process

above could also help identify suspicious entries or information that might identify fraud in the future. This is also where threat hunting could take place to identify potential issues or concerns.

4. Fast-Track Process - Through my many and extensive working relationships with law enforcement at all levels, there were times that law enforcement were tied up with other responsibilities and/or cases. Through discussions with several prosecuting offices, I was able to get agreement on certain fast-tracking of case components if those components were written in the acceptable format as deemed appropriate by the prosecutor. This also enabled some law enforcement contacts allowing me to proceed with certain investigations where time was of the essence because of certain circumstances and then catch up when possible. This won't be possible in all jurisdictions and environments, but you never know until you try.

5. Law enforcement relationships are very important, especially if you are involved in specific investigations responsibilities at your organization. Participating in industry groups is also helpful to gain contacts outside your jurisdiction and country.

Glossary

Term	Description
Asset Inventory	An enterprise-wide inventory of all assets, their functions, and their owners. The inventory should include a breakout of critical assets to better prioritize when dealing with incidents, business continuity, and disaster response. This is a fundamental concept of security and included as a basic requirement of many compliance frameworks.
AUP	Acceptable Use Policy - a way to provide an enforceable policy or standard for an organization of the "acceptable" uses allowed of corporate networking resources, including Internet use.
CCTV	Closed-Circuit Television - used for visibility of public and private areas within your organization. Newer systems will be in digital format with the use of digital video recording (DVR) systems and, in some cases, could be connected via Internet protocol (IP) over your network.

Chain of Custody	A process in which documentation exists that explicitly details the total control and custody of evidence from beginning to end. In the case of conducting civil and/or criminal investigations, the use of chain of custody is vital to the outcome of the prosecution of the individual involved in the case, especially when critical evidence exists.
DLP	Data Loss Prevention - tools, people, and processes that can be used in conjunction with one another for the purposes of ensuring your data security strategy for your organization. In a technology sense, DLP capabilities are offered through many tools and technologies, either stand-alone solutions or within existing tools with capability of performing DLP functions.
DOS/DDOS	Denial of Service/Distributed Denial of Service - most widely used name for attacks between one or more individuals targeting another individual or entity. There are various tactics and techniques that can be used to carry out either a DOS or DDOS. The outcome of either is to "deny" service so that the target cannot perform their service which could result in monetary loss, consumer confidence, and other hazards.
GDPR	General Data Protection Regulation - tied to privacy legislation in European Union countries that dictate consumer-data privacy in relation to its use by others, like a website. GDPR is just one of many country, nation, and/or state privacy bill/ regulation that dictates privacy law.

IOT	Internet of Things - the world in which we live is made up of many interconnected devices called the Internet. There are not just computers anymore, but now we have smart devices, medical devices, personal devices, home automation, and the list goes on. Anything that can connect to the Internet is considered IOT.
ISMS	Information Security Management System - essentially a set of policies and procedures for protecting an organization's sensitive data.
ISP	Internet Service Provider
PCAP	Contain packet data or PCAP files captured over network can contain network activity, uploaded files, requests made on websites (HTTP), etc.
PCI-DSS	Payment Card Industry - Data Security Standard - information security standard mandated by the credit card brands regarding minimum requirements to achieve compliance for PCI or those organizations handling payment transactions and consumer information connected to payment transactions
PMO	Project Management Office
SDLC	Secure Development Life Cycle
SIEM	Security Incident and Event Management - a tool (on premise or cloud-based) that helps support logging of critical devices, services, and applications for the purpose of security monitoring and detection of security events (based on predefined use cases) that require further investigation and remediation.

TSCM	Technical Surveillance Countermeasures - originating with the federal government denoting a process for sweeping for eavesdropping (bugs) and other devices.
Vulnerability Management	A framework used by an entity in the management of processes, policy, and technology (applications, software, and programs) used for scanning of your internal and external IP addresses representing your network infrastructure and/or applications to ensure vulnerabilities are identified, patched, and remediated to reduce the attack surface.

www.ingramcontent.com/pod-product-compliance
Lightning Source LLC
Chambersburg PA
CBHW051056050326
40690CB00006B/736